Howard Feather has taught social theory at the University of East London, City University, London and London Metropolitan University and is the author of *Intersubjectivity* and *Contemporary Social Theory: the Everyday as Critique*. He was a longstanding member of the Editorial Collective of the journal Radical Philosophy. He currently teaches sociology at the Open University.

To my mother, Hilda Feather (née Wilson), for her support and encouragement.

Howard Feather

SOCIAL THEORY OF DISPLACEMENT: ADVENTURES IN THE EVERYDAY

AUSTIN MACAULEY PUBLISHERS™

LONDON * CAMBRIDGE * NEW YORK * SHARJAH

A CIP catalogue record for this title is available from the British Library.

ISBN 9781398481190 (Paperback)
ISBN 9781398481206 (ePub e-book)

www.austinmacauley.com

First Published 2024
Austin Macauley Publishers Ltd®
1 Canada Square
Canary Wharf
London
E14 5AA

I am grateful to Merilyn Moos for her comments on the manuscript which proved invaluable in helping to clarify my thoughts. A debt is also owed to the work of members of the Radical Philosophy Collective and to Stella Sandford, Chris Arthur and Peter Hallward in particular. None of the above are responsible for errors that may have occurred in the writing.

Profound thanks are also due to Liz for her support during the period spanning the production of the text and for help with the preparation of the manuscript.

Table of Contents

Preface

The book originated in a series of essays and papers linked by the theme of displacement and which had been written over a number of years. These pieces were reworked and interlinked in the light of a theoretical framework which is elaborated in the introduction and first two chapters and which provides an underlying unifying account of displacement in the text.

Introduction

There was this chap called Max Stirner...[who] believed it would be alright if only we could get away from the tyranny of abstract ideas. (Anthony Powell, *Books do Furnish a Room*).

'Now nothing but Spirit rules the world' said the post – Hegelian Max Stirner but he could not elucidate it. Instead he blamed our 'fixed ideas', as if the fault were in us. But the fault is in reality. (Arthur, 2001, p.41).

The experience of displacement is one of ending up in a different place from that which was originally anticipated. This discrepancy between intentionality and actuality may be a cause for reflection where the prevailing reflective experience is of an unsettling or disorientating kind as suggested, for example, by the experience of a displaced person.

Again, switches in context or situation, and their points of reference, viewed in linguistic terms, as involving displacement of one term by another, can be seen as an unsettling dislocation or interruption of a line of thinking, and as a way of generating new meanings.

The focus here on the everyday, its 'wild logos'[1] of interrelatedness rather than hierarchical subsumption, and its critical, problematic relation to formal social systems and rationality lends another perspective to displacement. Here 'systemic' rather than accidental kinds of displacement is the concern; the displacement of informal interactional experiences[2] through their mediation via

---

[1] Merleau-Ponty, M. (1992a, pp. 102–3, 139).

[2] Here 'interaction' doesn't imply a relationship between two or more discrete individuals but takes the term to include interrelations between individuals and collectivities, where the individual is always a situated entity, that is, embodies their situation and hence communication between individuals is never purely between them

formal organisational structures of modern capitalism. Accordingly, it is argued, displacements in the realm of the experiential reveal functional, constitutive lacunae or voids in formal institutional practice and knowledge. These 'naturalise' formal institutional systems as discrete, autonomous realities in relation to the social practices which produce and reproduce them.

At the same time, the lacunae are nonetheless filled, invisibly, as agents actualise, operationalise formal bureaucratic structures in the here and now. Hence despite their invisibility, displacement in formal discourse itself, processes of actualisation remain in some way constitutive of the social order, its 'constitutive outside'.[3]

Before we turn to examine case studies, it will be necessary to engage in some conceptual throat clearing.

Theoretical Framework

The application of formal rules of state or market, the subsumption of people, events and things to formal rationality and its equivalencing of the particular, unique aspects of the lived world is characteristic of modernity. However, obversely formal rationality can only be actualised via a *modus operandi* which gives such structures of subsumption an anchorage in particular situations, conferring a quality of haecceity through which subsumption operates, and mobilises social life. Nevertheless, it is argued, in the process the living concrete world through which subsumption functions is displaced, rendered invisible by the moment in which life is subject to subsumption/abstraction vis a vis both market valorisation and formal organisational structures and their rationalising processes. Skills and artefacts appear as money values, individuals as roles or personhoods. Focussing on this state of affairs moves the discussion beyond an idea of displacement as the substitution of one term or representation by another and politically, further than hegemonic manoeuvres where power switches its circuits or classes compete, rise and fall.

The idea of displacement entertained here is then closer to a notion of ideology critique where misrecognition is the key to any discursive analysis.

---

as individuals in the sense of an homo economicus etc.

[3] For a useful discussion of this in relation to the reproduction of modern capitalism see Jessop, B (2006, p.165).

Here a number of signature traits might be encountered: a jarring of identifications, disorientation, alienation, confusion, the uncanny, a false sense of immediacy, colonisation, dualisms in thought and practice, and so on. Rather than suggest that misrecognition results from illusions anchored in individuals by the 'real effects' of ideological apparatuses or the overdetermination of one sign by another ('race' for class etc.), it is argued that it issues from the confusion of different realities, the world of lived experience and the world of real abstractions within which it gets subsumed. Here one ontological realm is being taken for the other. This may involve the idea of displacement as overdetermination of one sign by another but the crucial element for understanding the phenomenon of displacement we are seeking here is that one form of reality is confused with, appears in the guise of, and is equivalenced with, the other.

It is argued that the subsumption of lived, interactional relations, within formal institutional structures, as a contractualisation and/or commodification of them, is a form of abstraction. Further, the intertwining or mutual overdetermination of legal and economic factors is commonly taken to be characteristic of this real abstraction. The shared feature given in various accounts, Simmel (2011), Sohn-Rethel (1978), Arthur (2001), Halewood (2013), and Toscano and Bhandar (2015) seems to be property relations in modern bourgeois societies. The latter (op. cit., p.9) notes the role of

> private property…in dissolving social and communal relations, or at the very least in positing them as internal to a 'property logic' and the specificity of legal abstractions as…necessary…for the emergence of modern capitalism.

Hegel (1942, pp.62–3, 194) provides an account of a cognate idea. He notes the equivalencing of particular state services via money as the only way in which services can be judged to be commensurate. This quantification works

> only if these services are reduced to terms of money, the really existent and universal value of both things and services…in fact; however, money is not one particular type of wealth amongst others but the universal form of all types so far as they are expressed in an external embodiment and so can be taken as 'things'. Only by being translated into terms of this extreme culmination of externality can services be fixed quantitatively (ibid., pp.194–5).

Here the money relation has no determinate content and is quite arbitrary in relation to the concrete content of those services; an 'extreme' form of 'externality' in relation to their content. Although an abstraction, Hegel nonetheless takes the money relation as a real relation. These characteristics also epitomise the notion of property relations in the accounts given above. Hence a key element of displacement is evident here, the equivalencing of abstractions with sensuous particulars such that the former is confused with appears in the guise of the latter.

Because property relations connote both state and capital (including market transactions) they include contractualisation of social relationships and hence the whole sphere of formal institutional life and its consequent impact on hegemonic culture as a way of seeing how individuals are/should engage with each other in everyday life. The bureaucratic compartmentalisations of formal institutional life have an essential reflexivity where, for example, formal '…accounts are socially organised features of their use' (Garfinkel, 1967, pp. 3–4) and thus the suppressions of agents' situational improvisations of formal requirements appear discursively as relational voids.[4] In this way, the absence of agents' informal practices is naturalised as a dominant mode of experience.

Eminently, Habermas (1999) has pointed to this process in terms of an invasion of the life world of reciprocal, peer-based interactional relationships by contractual instrumental values of the 'system world' of modern capitalism.

Following on from this line of thought, we arrive at a sense of displacement peculiar to the interaction between the world of lived experience and that of market and contract abstractions where there is a confusion of the latter with the world of sensuous particulars, of lived experience. This is in fact prefigured in Kant's notion of subreption in his *Inaugural Dissertation* which 'designate(s) the confusion of sensible concepts with those of the understanding', or in an earlier account 'the error of illegitimately transferring concepts between different bodies of knowledge', a transgressive move which leads to forms of cross-

---

[4] See Feather (2016), p. 332 on bureaucratic construction of academic discourse as featured in its antinomialist tendencies: an emphasis on difference/identitarianism, micro-macro, modern-postmodern, resistance to inter- or trans-disciplinarity, and so on. In Capital, Marx notes the transformation of concrete productive activity into 'non-being' or nothingness whilst the empty equivalencer; 'value' becomes its 'being', a situation denoted by confusion or derangement, Verrückung (Arthur, op. cit., pp. 36, 42, n. 12).

fertilisation, new forms of knowledge (Howard, 2014, pp.49–50). Both of these ideas will be productive for a comprehensive grasp of subreption and hence displacement. The latter more conventionally recognised sense of displacement which will provide a useful contrastive device obversely signifies displacement as transference from one field of reference to another. That is, as suggested above, subreption can entail a confrontation between concepts/fields which leads to a paradigm shift, the transfer of a topic to a different field of reference.

On the other hand, the former possibility is taken up by Sandford (2011, p.29), see Chapter 2, in her examination of how of ideological effects of cognitive confusion in the classification of individuals according to sex produces a naturalisation of classification. 'Sex' appears at one and the same time as both particular (sex as a characteristic of the body) and as universal (a theory about the categorisation of bodies).

Here one meaning overlays, appears in the guise of the other, signifying a conceptual jarring or 'juddering'; a vacillation between biology and culture (Sandford, op. cit., p.29). The experience of vacillation or *vaciller* is investigated below in Lacanian (Duroux/Miller, 2012) theory of the subject, Barthes' critique of readerly discourse and in accounts of catachresis. The subreptive dimension of *vaciller* where abstractions appear as concrete particulars is viewed in the present discussion in terms of a colonisation of particulars by real abstractions where institutional subsumption of particulars within formal rationality occurs. Formal institutions, as Simmel (1978, p.78), notes regarding the economy, exist as abstractions; the economy 'is constituted by a real abstraction from the comprehensive reality of valuations', although, as argued above they are operationalised in the lived practices of the everyday.

The possible outcomes of *vaciller*, are, it is suggested here, as per Kantian subreption, twofold: on-going classificatory confusion where abstractions appear as concrete particulars, or, the translation of the non-subsumable particular to a new field of reference or paradigm as is variously argued by Sandford, Barthes, Duroux/Miller et al. This relies however on the presence of a contesting framework of ideas to break the on-going classification crisis.

As Barthes (2004, p.81), Sandford (2011, p.27) *et al.* have noted, such translations or displacements take the ordinary, everyday nature of some sign, person or artefact as their basis. This entity, normally taken for granted, is, given its multifaceted situatedness, polysemic, and it is its polysemy that acts as a basis for new translations. Whatever is taken as a point of departure here, moved on from, displaced, becomes the sedimented ground or taken for granted of the new field of reference or paradigm. It confers validity, recognition on the translations in the commonsense world of situated experience, it anchors signification in the everyday.

Translation

In the following discussion, translation is taken to be both discursive and occurring in space and time, and following the Chicago School is seen as occurring routinely in the movement of people, ideas and things between different social worlds

> ...a social world [is broadly]...a unit or set of interactions...not confined by geography or formal membership but rather is...an assemblage with shared commitments and practices (Carter et al. 2008, pp.4–5)

The interactions which take place in everyday life are symbolically informed and indicate, as Strauss (1978), Clarke (1997) et al. suggest, the openness and interpenetration of our different social worlds and importantly the interpenetration of their formal and informal aspects. This suggests a degree of reciprocity between agents in the negotiation of institutional life (Strauss, 1964) and therefore, the potentially transgressive nature of these forms of interrelation. The idea of social life as an on-going production, via its overlapping and multiply-occupied social worlds gives an underlying sense of diversity and hybridity/synthesis to translation in these accounts. Moreover, because of this sense of unity in diversity or the synedochal structure of such displacements it will be argued that the discursivity of social practice can be understood as a process of metaphorisation of social relations.

Metaphorisation as Social-Symbolic Translation

Sandford (2011) and du Gay (1997) have drawn on the transdisciplinary nature of translations anchored in everyday understandings in order to explain the processes behind shifts between fields of reference. The key discursive figure here is arguably that of metaphor and its synecdochal relations, how the figure suppresses some meanings in order to articulate others. In line with this metaphoric transfer, the translation of a word between different fields of reference; entails drawing on the doxa of the word's significations and establishing an articulation of this within a new field of reference

> The word is applied to a category different from that originally or normally designated by it and in which the ground of the transfer is some perceived similarity between the two categories (Waldron, 1967, p.162).

Translation is, therefore, a process of combining the familiar and the different. The different is grounded in aspects of the familiar. du Gay (1997, p.14) gives the example of the Sony Walkman as an object that emerges from the application of aspects of 'semantic networks' that apply to stereo, headphone, and cassette player to a new field of reference emphasising mobile listening: the new identification 'only works if you know the words 'stereo', 'headphone and 'cassette player'; these words are used 'metaphorically'.

Elsewhere Sandford discusses the ambiguity of 'sex' between biology and culture and how the contested nature of the term leads to or embodies a hiatus between a biological description and the (cultural) doxa such that an understanding of 'sex' requires a hybridisation of disciplines, a 'transdisciplinary problematic', the incorporation of hitherto submerged aspects of ordinary usage in a new identification or object. The metaphorisation of 'sex' is required. As Sandford (op cit., p.29) puts it:

> The transdisciplinary problematic arises in the relation between conceptual generalities…and the everyday linguistic usage, experiences and practices…

This translation arguably works by drawing on the suppressed cultural associations of the category 'sex' (its doxa) which *inter alia* ground the concept[5]. Here the practice of 'sex' moves or metaphorises the category as use of the category draws on a new field of reference which acknowledges its biological/cultural hybridity. Crucially here the sense of a new object/topic 'sex' is picked out by practice within this field of associations. As Waldron (loc. cit.) notes this works because

---

[5] The paradoxical consequences of attempting to separate biology and culture into two hermetically sealed categories are discussed in Chapter 2.

There is...some resemblance between what is normally designated by the word...and what is normally designated by its metaphorical use; its actual referent.

In other words, the conventional meaning, a placeholder, serves as point of departure for the metaphorical or discursive practice which hybridises the biological definition of the category translating the term 'sex' into a new field of reference.

Colonisation of Lived Reality

As Habermas (1999, p.174) has noted, within the domain of modern capitalism situated experience is subject to a colonising tendency of its lived quality where it is read through forms of commodification or the instrumental rationality of formal institutions. Instrumental rationality invades, hides within the 'lifeworld' and 'the illusion of its self-sufficiency' is maintained. The appearance of reciprocity of peer-to-peer relations, trust and transparency seems intact but this is a 'deception' pursued via an invisible parasitic relationship between system and lifeworld. It distorts perception such that individual concrete entities appear as types (ibid., pp.174–5).

Here displacement, as an invasion of the lived experience of everyday life, takes on a different inflection from the processes of translation described above. It rather follows, to use the framework of this book, the route of *vaciller* as abstractional subsumption where lived experience is confronted, equivalenced and 'appropriated' in a double-take style by the real abstractions of market and contract.

It is argued here that there are clear reasons why the subreptive impact of real abstractions is so seductive. Such subreption presents us with things that appear immediate, obvious, polar, natural and so on, and it does so by drawing on the doxa or sedimented grounds of the culture whilst presenting the latter as something universally valid, external to lived relations. The institutional appropriation of the notion 'sex' for example, results, as Sandford (2011, p.27) argues, in a dichotomous, characterisation where identities are unmediated, natural and desire is polarised. In this way, institutional abstractions are presented as sensuous particulars and conversely sensuous particulars appear as universally valid.

The trope of ideological effectivity in *vaciller* here is a way of working through the notion of colonisation and can be illustrated as follows. If the lived reality of sex is represented as a universal category; 'sex', then 'sex' appears as a generality which subsumes other sensuous particulars which it equivalences. Hence this form of equivalencing transforms or recruits concrete entities into abstract categories which then subsume or piggyback on other concrete entities within a given order of signification and its associations or connotative chains. (This discussion is taken up again in Chapter 3 in relation to commodification of the body).

Thus the lived reality of sex and its doxic elements, associations can be deployed over a range of connotations such as gendered forms of bodily conduct, identity, consumption, and so on, in such a way that they are all essentially 'sex' where 'sex' functions as a placeholder that condenses and 'articulates' a range of connotative elements as manifestations of 'sex'.[6] This exemplifies how the metaphoric figure of 'sex' as a form of everyday usage and translation has been hijacked as an abstractional object for, in Kant's terms, 'an object in the idea', as Sandford notes, (op. cit., p.28) on the vacillation between classifications and empirical objects in Kant. As *vaciller* the synedochal part-whole relation of the metaphorical translation is frozen such that whatever connotations the part-whole figure suppresses become indefinitely inaccessible rather than in process of finding an articulation in lived experience, a translation to a new field of reference, or social world.

This *vaciller* without subsumption/articulation means that there is an ongoing subreptive confusion of categories (male/female) with lived bodily experience which, as suggested, indicates that synthesis, cross-fertilisation and translation do not take place, that the hybridity of identities, the fact that they are always already a synthesis of different influences, as subreption suggests, is suppressed. There is, in the suppression therefore a definite displacement, a colonisation of lived experience where one thing, the abstraction, passes itself off, is equivalenced with, another whilst gaining its force from this. In so doing, the abstraction appears as separate from social relations and is hence naturalised;

---

[6] See Hall, S. (1986) for an account of displacement as condensation or a summary of this in Feather (2000), pp.63–4. The resemblance to metaphorical displacement is noteworthy. The latter may arguably involve, in our case, elements ranging from medical science, gender relations, including their media constructions, to constructions of desire, and so on.

an 'extreme form of externality', in Hegel's terms. It is arguably this form of displacement which characterises capitalist modernity.

Appropriation

It can be seen that subreptive confusion takes the discussion beyond colonisation in its Habermasian guise and raises important questions for a common trope of cultural analysis – appropriation. From the above discussion, it becomes clear that appropriation is not a seamless process and that informal interactional life is displaced, mimicked here rather than transformed in a genuine synthesis. This point is reinforced by the paradox that cultural analysts continue to identify a cultural content that has been appropriated as a commodity as if it hadn't been! Appropriation in this form requires both transformation of an artefact, style of music, for example, and a continuing recognition of what has been commoditised. Hence it is not as though there is a cultural 'ping-pong' in which say, individuals customise commodified products and relations only for the system to re-appropriate these innovations in the form of commodities (Feather, 2018, p.122). In other words, there is no symmetry here and hence, no justification of a tendency towards fatalism in cultural analysis because as the discussion will go on to suggest, the everyday of informal practice doesn't cease to exist, is not annihilated when system appropriation occurs, it rather co-exists relatively inaccessibly. The displacements or 'residuum' of modern capitalism therefore continue to accrete, rather than having to start from scratch, so to speak, every time informal practices customise rationalised and commodified content of experience. This lends a different perspective to the potential offered by customisation of this content.[7]

---

[7] See Husserl (1970, pp. 361–2) for an account of sedimentation and the reactivation of this residuum, which suggests an enduring positivity of this displaced content. See also the discussion in Chapter 4 of displaced or 'worn-away' metaphor, which 'acts behind our backs' and how it can be re-enlivened or re-articulated to convey its on-going sense in the here and now.

1

Displacement and Translation

This chapter will explore the phenomenon of displacement through the idea of translation. Displacement as translation can be broken down into a number of key aspects. These would include its perceptual, psychoanalytic, linguistic and sociological dimensions. These will now be outlined both in terms of what translation would look like if uninhibited by real abstractions (Dynamic, negotiated reciprocity, a social relations of mutual recognition) and what happens when it is (dichotomies, hiatuses in discursive practices, fragmentation of social relations, confusion, incomprehension, misrecognition, disorientation, spectrality of lived relations, the uncanny, alienation, and so on).

In this way, we can both see the mechanisms of translation as operating as unimpeded by the strategies of appropriation (Commodification and contractualisation, for example) basic to modern capitalism and contrastively when appropriation does occur. We thus gain a perspective on the contested nature of experience in this milieu and hence on the impact of modernity as expressed in a *vaciller* of the subject.

Chapters 1 and 2 set the scene for the following discussions on cultural hegemony, language and power, capitalism and networks. This chapter begins by looking at some familiar signature traits of displacement but within the framework of translation. These are dualism, the experience of exile/self-alienation and an interpretation of the concept 'suture'. Chapter 1 then goes on to summarise some key perspectives though which translation in these instances might be understood.

Signature Traits of Displacement

Dualism

The discursive-institutional formations of modern life indicate a hiatus in which interrelation and processes are considered as separate from social structure. This feature is closely linked to the instrumental rationality which Weber and others have seen as characteristic of formal institutional life in the modern world.

This does not only suggest deficiencies in our knowledge of social reality but more significantly also indicates this abstractional quality is an objective part of knowledge/social practice/organisational structure in modernity.

Bureaucratic and market fragmentation of lived relations divorces process and practice from outcomes. Writings as various as Lukács (1971, pp.88–92) on reification and Foucault (1982, pp. 118–119) on the production of 'gaps' or 'voids' in the enunciative field (*rarifaction*) supports the view that gaps in formal knowledge/practice, are in fact, constitutive of the social order demarcated by formal institutional processes. Markets and specialisation in the division of labour can be seen as overlapping and mutually reinforcing processes of fragmentation which delimit what can be said or made visible.[8] More recently Arthur (2001) has described capital as an abstractional relation voiding the creative process of living labour and Barthes (2004, pp. 9–23) has discussed the hollowing out of contextual meanings in formal or readerly ('syllogistic') discourse.

Whether living language or labour, these grounding contextual, taken for granted meanings might generally be equated with a culture's sedimented resources, those spontaneous understandings that shape our current focus. However, when these are located in a dualistic mode of apprehension, their dislocation from praxis gives them a hypostatised, naturalised tenor, they convey a sense of reality as something autonomous, complete in itself and immediately given, tangible yet abstract-relating the force of generality to our particular experiences through which they become more real than real, a semblance of concreteness in world of abstractions (Halewood, 2013, p. 159),[9] arguably a hyper-reality. A corollary of this point is that any sense of process, mediation of

---

[8] 6 See sections on Lukács, Rancière and Hayek in Ch 5 for development of this point.

[9] The notion of a misplaced concreteness is attributed by Halewood to A.N. Whitehead's *Science and the Modern World*.

outcomes by their grounding point of departure is lost (ibid., pp.162–5 and Ch.8, *passim*).

By contrast, it is suggested, a sedimented culture which connects with our situation and enlivens it as its common sense, and as its self-reflection, casts light on our praxis. A useful example might be women's emancipation in the 1960s–70s, which connects with and enlivens today's experiences of gender-based oppression and renders feminism once more the recognisable name of a cause/situation. This situating perspective can be opposed to a stageist or progressionist, more compartmentalised, 'bureaucratic' view which might suggest we've 'moved on' and left concerns with the collective experience of women at work etc. behind in favour of a post-feminism that accentuates individual advancement, traditional strategies in gender conflict, and so on.

Such 'stageism' sets up a dualism of past-present stages where translation as differentiation is the key process in arriving at a new field of reference for feminism. This model can be applied to other areas such as those of academic disciplinary compartmentalisation of different approaches to the same topic area where a kind of antinomialism takes the place of dialogics and interdisciplinarity (Feather, 2016, pp. 328–9).

However, by using for example, the model of translation as metaphoric transfer discussed above as critique it can be seen that any differentiation requires a moment of dialogics or synthesis where elements of the original field of reference undergo (as 'raw materials'), a switch in reference in the presence of new fields. This transfer requires a common ground, a point of connection between the fields, a moment of resemblance or perceived similarity (Waldron, 1967, p.167ff). As we have argued, the outcome of translation cannot be detached from a synthesis with the everyday, that is, the process through which it is arrived at, even if as with a bureaucratic stageism this moment gets displaced from the terrain of the visible, and gives the emerging category a misplaced concreteness, absolute difference – conveyed by 'we've move on' etc.

(Chapters 2 and 3 will *inter alia* examine how the lived experience of women, drawing on sedimented practice, enables them to question the reification and sequestration of their identities in modern capitalism).

Gaps, compartmentalisations or differences translate organisationally as disciplinary, areas of specialism, a division of labour and so on, in the bureaucratic sense outlined here. Ethnomethodologists have argued (see Cuff, Sharrock et al., 1992, p.176, for example) that such gaps are under continuous repair through agents' activities although the latter are not generally perceived as structural/intrinsic features of organisational life but rather seen as a kind of add-on through which organisational life is made to run more smoothly.[10]

The organisational emphasis on acting as teams and on teamwork (see Chapter 5) is one example of how in fact day-to-day coordination is routinely seen as a contingent way of improving operations rather than 'something that goes on all the time' yet remains invisible as a feature of organisational structure. Goffman's (1982, pp. 83–108) work on this acknowledges the ontological status of teamwork as everyday rather than formal management policy. Teamwork is displaced from, and remains invisible to, the sensorium of formal organisational life but nevertheless exists, to repair the operational gaps in the visible, formal structures. Hence individuals' social situatedness appears as contingent rather than an intrinsic organisational feature. A gap is thus opened up between individuals and organisations, and also consequently been the latter and (invisible) agential coordination of different organisational functions and likewise for the coordination of different organisations.

Institutional projects are nevertheless operationalised. To understand how a social order can be simultaneously both fragmented and exhibit continuity/coherence we need to introduce the idea of different but intertwined ontological orders or domains, something evident in writers such as Husserl (1970), Schutz (1970a), Habermas (1999), Lefebvre (2002), de Certeau (1984) and Goffman (1982). As we have argued, in capitalist modernity actors exist in both an everyday world of lived experience or lifeworld and in formal, abstract systems and these two aspects of social reality are interdependent. Action in the lifeworld can appropriate aspects of the world of formal organisations/rationality and vice versa. The formal system world can in Habermas's (1999) term 'colonise' the lifeworld[11] where agents are interpellated as bearers or functionaries of system imperatives. These are different but linked ontological domains where one forms the invisible ground of the other and under specific situational conditions this relation can undergo a reversal rendering the previous ground the visible topic

---

[10] See Giddens (2001) for an account of structure – agency dualism in sociology. The present author would not necessarily agree with Giddens' solution, structuration theory, but Giddens highlights dualism as a major issue in the discipline.

[11] Colonisation of the lifeworld is a key feature of abstraction in this discussion, where relations of market and state abstract or derive their 'life' and subsumptional discursive power from the world of lived reciprocal relations.

(ibid., p.171). Hence we may view the system world whilst bracketing the world of lived experience and vice versa. It is argued here that the world of lived experience is largely invisible within dominant forms of discursive practice, dissociated from formal organisations. Habermas's topology of system and life world may itself accentuate a dualistic perspective in that systems are seen to possess their own (autonomous) dynamic (Feather, 2000, pp. 39–40, 44–5).

Displacement as exile

Dualism also impacts on the experience of the individual subject in the sense that modernity is encountered as a form of self-estrangement which atomises subjects, they appear as asocial, external both to themselves and to others, exiles from their collective life. Writers such as Jameson (1989) and MacIntyre (2007) have noted how the state bureaucracy individualises members of social groups such that they seem inexplicably simultaneously connected and disconnected.

Although this section focuses on the state and its institutions, it is important to note that this political entity is inextricable from economic life. The state is economic as well as juridical. The modern state is the locus of exchange in the sense that exchange is predicated on the juridical – property relations, contracts. In a marketised economy, the capacity to labour is sold in the labour market and thereby becomes, via contract, possession guaranteed by the state – the property or capital of the purchaser. Here particular endeavours are equivalenced via contractual market relations. The productions of labour are therefore the production of property in the form of capital – of intertwined state and market relations.

These relations individualise in the sense that services, as the above discussion of Hegel noted, appear as external to any intrinsic/use value the individual possesses in relation to the collective. The individual is presented to themselves as an abstraction – a provider of services equivalenced with other abstract providers rather than the services that relate to their specific situational use/need. As Hegel argued, here the exchange appears as external to intrinsic characteristics of concrete services. The individual who provides them therefore experiences themselves as external to the social relations of context, ties to collectivity and hence experiences themselves as de-situated, and thus atomised.

Hegel's point is not simply that we are de-centred, experience ourselves as defined by others, but that the abstraction of equivalencing here represents a qualitatively different ontological terrain where the individual is interpellated in (state) contractual form as radically separate, external to the collectivity – 'an extreme externality' (see Introduction).

Thus the state, for example, confronts us as Sayer (Halewood, op. cit., p. 160) argues, not as members of communities, networks, peers and so on, but as 'abstract' individuals, '*citoyens*' only in this sense. We are members of a world which is both familiar and strange, and so disorienting. As with the popular album title[12] we are 'exiles on main street': at once, for example, negotiating the metropolis as concrete adventure, the novel experience, and at the same time subject to its other face, the interweaving forms of abstract exchange. It is this sense of exile/displacement as cognitive confusion or *vaciller* which characterises *inter alia*, urban experience.

The state, in its externality, seems to precede society, contra the Aristotelian vision of communal virtue enabling the state (Jameson, 1989, p.182). Rationalisation via market and contract produces a culture of bureaucratic individualism (ibid., p.183) in which we emerge/subtend as strangers to ourselves.[13]

As Schutz (1970b, p.109) has argued, the corollary of this formal rationality is that it always carries with it a cultural 'subscript', a marker of situational relevance through which its abstractions can be applied. Hence whilst formal subsumption displaces the particularity of the individual this haecceity of situation nonetheless continues to function silently as a way of operationalising abstractions in the here and now, as noted in the Introduction. In the case of the state, it functions against those not culturally situated by it. These individuals find negotiating this invisible logic relatively difficult compared to those steeped in its assumptions.

An extreme case of state subsumption as individualisation is located by Moos (2015) who has argued that refugees and their descendants face a radical disconnect where they are divorced from their own experiences: their cultural identities, memories, biographies, narratives and their historical past cannot be easily rearticulated through a present linked to a subscript cultural identity sanctioned by different state.

Another example of the abstraction of individuals as contractual subjects, that is, contractually equivalenced individuals, is the interpellation of black

---

[12] 'Exile on Main Street', The Rolling Stones, 1972.

[13] Jameson is here discussing MacIntyre's (2007) relation between the community and the polis.

senior civil servants within an ostensibly neutral state apparatus (examined in Chapter 3). Puwar (2004, p.113) observes that the 'educational spaces (such as public schools and Oxbridge)' are a key element of what's been referred to above as the cultural subscript through which interpellation occurs. Arguably, 'Oxbridge'/public school is here a cultural identifier colonised by the state to confer legitimacy on its activities.

These colonised apects of culture are expressed as naturalised by the fragmenting impact of formal subsumpton as is shown in Scarry's account which illustrates how attributes of lived culture are reflected back by subsumption as fixed ('universal') definers of belonging. Scarry (1985, pp.108–9) notes.

> The extent to which–the nation-state resides unnoticed in the intricate recesses of personhood, penetrates the deepest layers of consciousness and manifests itself in the body itself is hard to assess...[It] seems at many moments ... *there* in the learned postures, gestures, gait, disposition of the tongue, mouth, throat [and indeed in the whole body language of the individual – H.F.].

This makes it difficult for the outsider to articulate their own cultural formation through this already present apparatus of communication. Hence a form of displacement is enacted where the individual has to mimic the forms of a sutured, inaccessible, abstract/universal cultural formation rather than work through them as a natural mode of self-expression. The outsider subject experiences subsumption as a subreptive *vaciller*, the disorientation of being someone and yet not being that person.

State-sponsored identities can however be contested and displaced by informal, negotiated ('lifeworld') attachments where the individual negotiates their situation within the social formation through its voluntary cultural and political life where they cease to be sutured from the collectivity as Moos's (op. cit., p. 278) work attests in the case of her refugee father. His involvement in a local community cultural centre, and later, in other local writing groups positioned him outside his contractualised identity.

A sense of this contestability of formal identities is provided in Chapter 2 where Sandford's discussion of formal sexual identities and their confused nature as bicategorisation suggests *vaciller* provides the basis of contestation and of asserting lived identities to displace these formal, bureaucratic denominations.

Rustin and the Psychology of Internal Exile

It is worth turning to the psychology of displacement to look at how the suppression of articulation of lived experience impacts on the production of such discourse and its figures. The interpellation of subjects within formal bureaucratic discourse can have, depending on the contestation of such interpellations, as Rustin (2008) suggests, repressive implications for those engaged in the (re)production of such discourse as well as those interpellated as its clients; the public.

Whilst one would expect any formal classification system to typify the things, people or situations it deals with, institutional abstraction goes beyond this by equivalencing particulars in a way that fixes, naturalises them. This is seductive in the sense that it gives is subjects a kind of false immediacy, a way of dealing with the gaps and related anxieties left by abstractional subsumption. Hence, although Rustin deals with extreme cases and failures of institutional care systems, arguably the model can be applied to any formal institutional setting and its dynamics. Essentially, Rustin's discussion provides a way of understanding the link between abstraction and stereotyping, the interpellation of individuals as fragments, 'part objects' and so on. This topic is taken up in subsequent chapters.

A résumé of Rustin's discussion is as follows. Rustin (2008, p.172) has argued that fragmented organisational structures reinforce and are mutually constitutive of subjective states of in effect, internal exile, the borderline states of disengagement with 'external' realities. The fragmentation consequent on, for example, state services is mirrored in the inability of the individual to cope with crisis and engage with others except by a kind of bureaucratic non-relation, a closed (narcissistic) discourse, which displaces anxiety and make sense of the nonsensical situation by inventing a fictional narrative of blame as a kind of defence mechanism.

As Rustin (loc. cit.) argues, the individual and formal institutions coproduce abstractional, alienated, naturalised social forms: the bureaucracy individualizes and the individual bureaucratises; the individual's responses are formulaic and represent a psychic crisis to match the institutional hiatuses. The relational gaps in formal organisational structure are mirrored in the agent's inability to construct a coherent narrative of interrelation, moments of coordination are suppressed. Hence, in crisis situations organisational imperatives seem, via suppression of the living engagement with, concrete operation of, the organisation, to pass directly, as a form of paralysis, into the failure of agents' projects. Here the individual is confronted with a version of themselves they do not recognise. This is not a splitting of the individual from organisational life but a splitting of both into lived intersubjectivity and bureaucratised or abstractional 'life'. (The theme of institutional hiatuses is further explored in Chapters 3 and 5).

The gap presented by discursive failure; the ways of articulating interrelations meaningfully, Rustin argues, drives individuals and organisations into narcissistic or fractured states. Anxieties cannot be communicated and the objects of our inner worlds become 'damaged' or 'dead' (pp. 152, 154). These internal objects can then be projected onto the external world as bureaucratic reifications or stereotypes, forms of institutional rationalisation, but at the same time organisational articulations (displacements) of one's lived experience (ibid., p.172). As Rustin says, regarding the psychology of interrelational 'breakdown'.

States of mind usually associated with individuals can come to characterise ways in which members of an organisation…routinely relate to each other and to those with whom they come into contact (loc. cit.).

Thus the crisis is mutually constituted on and by individual and organisational levels as a fracturing of the intersubjectivity of social relations.

Whilst Rustin's (op. cit., pp.143–147) approach is not that of abstractional displacement in formal institutions the empirical content of his discussion focussing on institutions of health and social care indicates the hiatuses or voids in discursive practice which a displacement of lifeworld, that is, intersubjective features would suggest.

The discussion now moves on to look at ways in which such hiatuses and their vacillations might lead to productive outcomes, translations to new fields of reference and understanding.

Vaciller: From Abstraction and Dislocation to the Articulation of Lived Experience

The Suture

In general terms, 'suture' designates the closure of a discourse whilst at the same time it also indicates a destabilisation. A name, placeholder or cover concept, defining and closing a narrative, equivalencing its terms, is itself equivalenced by them and becomes a particular signifier, opening itself to other meanings. This oscillation between the particular and the general undermines the discourse's claims to closure and universality. This meaning instability generates an unlimited trail of signifiers in search of a referent.

Two contrastive approaches to suture are discussed in the following, one derived from a reading of Williams and Eagleton via the notion of abstraction developed above and the other derived from Lacan's idea of translating the analysand to a position of self-understanding which involves rearticulating the subject's position in/between orders of signification via interpellations of hitherto repressed experiences.

In consonance with the two preceding sections, it will be in order to begin with suture as entailing the abstractional and naturalising tendencies of discursive practices. This will then be used to preface ways in which genuine translations of discursive practices from one social world or field of reference to another can take place via articulation of lived experience.

In the present reading of Williams and Eagleton, 'suture' means the conjoining of antinomial discursive structures such that they feed off each other as a social dualism where lived practices and processes which mediate this apparent disjunction in discursive practice are displaced and the binary discursive structure is thereby naturalised.

Williams (1971, p.17), discussing industrialisation in the UK, locates the reception of this new mode of life in terms of its impact: as an understanding of culture 'as an abstraction and an absolute' as opposed to, and judgementally situated in relation to, 'the driven impetus of a new kind of society'.

Eagleton (1975, pp.93–101), drawing on Williams has identified the sensuous immediacy of narrative and concomitant idealisations of situation found in the literary canon of this emerging industrial capitalist social formation and which also carry through to the post-1945 period. This is picked out through a number of key themes as follows: Community versus 'solipsistic individualism'; 'single secret principle' for reading an 'artefact'; 'combines idealist totality' and 'sensuous empiricism…its other face'; 'collective unconscious' versus 'dislocative immediacy of its sensuous recreations'; a 'hard precise image which contains its concept'; 'the transmutation of thought into sense experience'; texts as 'closed systems which are directly coterminous with the world itself'; 'the work as radically closed to its audience [while] apparently communicating more exactly', and so on.

As mentioned above, this is a reading of Williams and Eagleton from the point of view of *vaciller* and abstraction and should be taken here as purely indicative in relation to the role of abstraction in cultural hegemony. Abstraction here is not about content so much as the form the content takes under real abstraction. The conjunction between sensuous immediacy and idealisation in the illustrations above resembles the conjunction of concrete and universal encountered in the discussion of *vaciller* where there is a failure of synthesis and translation, and instead, an equivalencing of objects with universals that echoes the abstractional processes of market and state practices. Today such processes might be identified in the euphoria of globalisation and hyperspace, the 'more real than real' of hyperreality or 'the spectacle', and, arguably, in the virtual concrete internet 'community'. The commercial internet suggests interconnectedness on a vast scale but its algorithms equivalence users with other users and products in abstract ways, suggesting a decontextualised immediacy which fits the explanatory model developed here.

As it was argued in the previous section, by suppressing the social mediations of cultural production the reader as subject is paradoxically interpellated via institutional modes of reception as external to the social and rather as coincident with the universal equivalencing of their sensuous experience, which denies the individual, situated character of their reading. (The generation of typologies of the abstract individual as reified personhoods or forms of *homo clausus* is discussed in Chapter 2).

As a postscript to this section, it should be noted that reading culture in this way, that is, in terms of the hiatuses of discursive practice is not necessarily to reject the fictive/metaphorical truthfulness of texts and readings of cultural artefacts. They are, after all, the performative expression of the social reality which is their medium. The literary text functions arguably in a similar way to myth in expressing the way contradictions of the social world are handled and negotiated. This provides, according to Levi-Strauss, a 'logical model' for 'overcoming contradiction' (Wood, 2017, p.22). Therefore, whilst on one level, as a hegemonic form of reading, the text embodies the lack of synthesis between universal and particulars, on another it articulates the lived experience of the reader. As such cultural artefacts can be seen to function as placeholders, sites for 'repair work', the displacement of contradictions in discursive practices.

This series of illustrations has characterised the abstractional form of *vaciller*. The discussion now turns to cases where subsumptive *vaciller*, the actual articulation of lived experience, the translation of the subject to a different field of reference is realised. Here, mediational processes between polarities is evident: cause and outcome, subject and structure/object exist relationally, they mediate each other. The following section will look at some perspectives on the process of translation between fields of reference or social worlds in social theory, enabling an appreciation of its centrality. It will, arguably, be seen from this that *vaciller* is also central to understanding the structure of social process.

Non-Abstractional *Vaciller*

Whilst in the above discussion we have noted a hiatus in aspects of discursive practice rather than a synthesis of ways of thinking and modes of practice, gaps or voids within the systemic operation of modernity, it has also been apparent that this 'lack' enables it to function. The lack in this case entails forms of misrecognition, a false sense of immediacy where topic or outcome is substituted for the mediating process via which it is arrived at.

It will now be argued that a lack in discourse/signification can also work in favour of connecting individuals with their (displaced) lived experience; the suppressed articulations of the subject's identity. The lack or hiatus in communication in this case is arguably not due to abstract equivalencing concrete things or values but to another kind of suppression, lack of articulation within discourse of the subject's lived experience and desire. As we have seen from Waldron (op. cit., pp.166–7) in the process of signification some metaphorical associations are suppressed and translation of the subject's situation may thereby be inhibited; the concept appropriate to articulating the subject's desire/experience may not be apprehended. Consequently, this lack does not necessarily indicate a colonisation of the subject's experience but rather an inability to name its topic through the absence of an appropriate field of reference or signification. However, the most socially significant trope of translation here is the contestation of colonisation whether this takes the form of challenging the division of labour or other mediations of market and state contractualisation.

In what follows, it is assumed for the sake of simplification that colonisation is not a factor and we survey what translation would look like without forms of abstractional subsumption/colonisation. Abstractional subsumption will be revisited in Chapter 2 and beyond. It suffices to say that as we have seen from the work of Sandford and Schutz, contesting and opening of systems of signification to their lived (doxic) conditions of possibility suggests that discursive lacunae can be productive of shifts in understanding. Under these circumstances the topic may be grasped indexically via partial or incomplete articulation and apprehended metaphorically; traced, hinted at, but not defined. Translation would require a contesting conceptual framework to identify and re-think the perplexities raised by the occurence of *vaciller*.

'Suture' Once More – A Lacanian[14] Reading

We now turn to psychoanalysis where this point is made by Miller (2012a) in his article 'Suture' where the suture is taken as the logic of the signifier as Hoens (2014, p.48) notes. Understanding how signification works requires 'first and foremost, sticking to the superficial plane on which signifiers operate and resisting the temptation of any depth psychology' that is, adhering to the level of conventional meanings and resisting interpretive urges. In this way, we can see the 'action of the structure in its effects'. In other words, the gaps in the logic of the system of signification and their function can be revealed, that is, the hiatuses that require interpretive (repair) work to make sense of the situation of application of the system of signification. In this manner, the illogicality of the system is revealed but it is also apparent that this symptomatic reading indicates via background information/context the nature of the displacement of the subject's identifications and the direction of a therapeutic translation.

Miller and Duroux employ Frege's idea that an illogical term is a necessary part of a logical order. Hoens (op. cit., p.49) notes that Frege's approach to logical order was based on the illogical concept 'not identical with itself'. This is described as an excluded content which is essential to the logic of the system, in this case arithmetic. Here zero is taken to be the excluded content of the integer, number one, and the whole of the rest of the arithmetical system therefore depends on this excluded content. Hence the number one, signifying unity, is not identical with itself.

---

[14] See Hallward, P. and Peden, K. (eds.), *Concept and Form*. Strictly speaking this is an appropriation of the work of Lacan and Althusser by the group associated with the journal *Cahiers Pour l'Analyse*.

Miller (loc. cit.) argues that the excluded content of any system of signification is 'always needed in order to make the structure operational' and that this is its weak point. This, in our perspective, is the point of operationalisation or interpretation; 'repair work'. That is, intervention regarding the contradictions and here

the logic of the signifier is fundamentally marked by a blank or a void (zero) represented by a placeholder that both indicates and covers up an inevitable exclusion.

For Lacanians (Duroux, op. cit., p.190 n.6), this is a content which is displaced or repressed from discourse. The placeholder is a 'lure' or 'decoy' which distracts the subject from its only partial articulation (interpellation) with actuality. This equivocation or vacillation (*vaciller*) between the actual and the plane of signification, that is, between content and its signification leads to a specific form of misrecognition. This can be described as follows. The concept/signifier is taken as the concrete content thus naturalising the signifier such that signification itself seem immediate, concrete and in this way, it mimics or 'redoubles' the concrete subject (ibid., p.189).

Conversely, the occluded content, as 'return of the repressed', interrupts the flow of meaning at this point of weakness in the structure. Hence this is the point where, as Duroux (2010b, p.193) observes, the formal structure or logic ('imaginary element') of the structure 'can be made to topple over (*basculer*)'. This is the 'topic point' of similarity or coincidence between discourse and the lived world and it is equally the point/place where they are differentiated or other, and therefore, where experience is opaque to discourse. The inability to subsume or signify the experiential world entails that its doxa 'appears', becomes coincident with the surface or conventional signifier, suffuses it, transforms its meaning, produces an opening onto the world.

As Duroux (op. cit., p.190) observes,

There is a point in the structure [of signification] which represents, which is the placeholder, precisely, of the point of lack in the structure itself. Analysis is precisely the detecting of this point; the utopic or the infinite point interpretation consists in grasping certain signifiers which weigh more than others, since it is on the basis of them that one might then reconstitute a chain of signifiers that remains unknown to the subject.

In Lacanian terms, this represents the possibility that 'the subject will be able to re-establish itself having traversed its *leurres* [lures] as so many symptoms' and so it indicates a transfer and interpellation within a different chain of signifiers (ibid., p.193). In other words, analysis enables a translation to a new field of reference. At a macro or cultural level, the eventuation of a *basculer* would require a generalised meaning crisis where the placeholder becomes a focus for multiple points of *vaciller*, a focus of the contradictions within the signifying order (ibid., pp.192–3).

Although this part of the discussion has worked through Lacanian/*Cahiers* symptomatic reading, it has also been intimated that the argument applies more generally to the way an order of signification is undermined and that there is a consequent perceptual switch induced by weaknesses indicated by a placeholder signifier. Here excluded content has the capacity to indicate something different from that which is routinely signified. The foregoing should therefore be seen as complementing rather than opposing the perspectives now to be outlined.

Perceptual Switch and *Gestalt* Theory: Going Beyond Psychologism

The switches in perception marked by a void in signification can be investigated via the work of Merleau-Ponty (1992a) who argues that this is not merely a subjective switch, a choosing of one field of reference over another but a point at which logic and reality overlap and hence a rearrangement of the situation of the subject.

In Hegel's sense, this is a logic of content. In other words, rather than the logical organisation of facts coming from a form that is superimposed on them, the very content of these facts is supposed to order itself spontaneously in a way that is thinkable (ibid., p.52).

This is achieved by collection of relational data as open systems or types. In this way, concrete experience is linked to reason. In other words, experience is perceived as interrelation, as intersubjective, rather than a closed analytic system. Therefore, experiences are grasped not merely as those of an isolated subject but as part of wider trends, that is, as the sense of the collective projects of which one's experiences are a part (ibid., pp.53–4). Hence, for example, we could talk about apprehending the logic of structures such as capital or hegemonic masculinity, or again, about body language, as shared content.

Thus Merleau-Ponty (op. cit., p.76) argues, following Kopff's *Principles of Gestalt Psychology*, that a change occurring in the interrelations of experience overlaps with a change taking place in the sensible world. In other words, having the experiences and the activity of experiencing, interconnect at some point. The Gestaltists held to

The notion of an order of meaning which does not result from the application of spiritual [i.e. intellectual – H.F.] activity to an external matter. It is, rather a spontaneous organisation beyond the distinction between activity and passivity, of which the visible patterns of experience are the symbol (ibid., p.77).

Hence in *Gestalt* psychology, meaning is already imbricated in perception; there is already a logic or organisation to the elements.

But this sense which inhabits all psychic phenomena, is not produced by a pure activity of spirit [i.e. intellect – H.F.]. It is, rather, an earthy and aboriginal sense, which constitutes itself by an organisation of the...elements (loc. cit.).

Therefore, 'psychology and logic do not belong to two domains of discourse, so basically different that no intelligible relation can exist between them' (ibid., p.76).

Elsewhere Merleau-Ponty describes this overlap between objectivity ('logic') and the subject as intentional transgression. It is the way our subjectivity is disrupted by the logic of its situation. My 'gaze' is 'thwarted' by 'certain sights', they produce me just when I thought I was constructing them. I experience my body as shaped by interactions with others and their point of view (Merleau-Ponty, 1998, p.94). Speech, which is 'an eminent case' of conduct is a means of 'revers[ing] my ordinary relationship to objects and gives certain ones of them the value of subjects'. The body is an incarnation of its thinking in its 'total speech' (loc. cit.). The body situates us in time and space. It is this situatedness through which the body overlaps with, interrupts the *Cogito* or self-enclosed unity of the thinking subject (ibid., p.95). Hence the *I* of the thinking subject is intersected by the *I* of the situated body. Thus the body offers a source of 'instructive spontaneity' (ibid., p.94) and encapsulates the ability to know the preconstituted world beyond my consciousness, as 'this life's incarnate thought' (ibid., p.95), in effect the body's progress or narration through time and space.

If we think of the everyday way individuals' lives are networked, we can see this both as intended pattern or logic of a constituting subject and as the objective structuring, situating of their lives. Hence the subject as constituted is not the subject of intentionality, rather this embodied subject carries with them a surplus of meaning; the 'total speech' of the incarnate subject.

It is this invisible surplus of meaning which forms the basis of the interruption or transgression of the intentionality of the conscious subject. This bracketed *(epoché)* content, as argued above, provides the means of operationalising formal systems, it gives context to what is otherwise an abstract, 'on paper', grasp of situation. It can also signify the point where nothing coherent can be said, the point where signification breaks down, the place where transgression results in translation to a new field of reference. For Merleau-Ponty, such a hiatus is the juncture at which an existing project ceases to make sense, has become disengaged from situation (Kruks, 1990, p.139). Translation is hence a re-engagement with situation.

Barthes: The Haiku and *Tremblé du Sens*

We will now turn to Barthes' version of *vaciller* because it encapsulates key features of the process as delineated in the discussion so far. The ordinary, everyday or insignificant is presented as a mode of interruption of signification and this is illustrated by the haiku as a vehicle of the 'shaking of meaning' or *tremblé du sens*. The haiku is a site of the void or 'emptiness of language' which constitutes the creative moment of writing. Hence the void, whilst a space or hiatus is not nothing, but an active phenomenon. The *tremblé du sens* is a 'Zen occurrence', following Barthes' illustrative construction of a 'Japan' figure.

This situation is the very one in which a certain disturbance of the person occurs, a subversion of earlier readings, a shock of meaning lacerated, extended to the point of its irreplaceable void, without the object's ever ceasing to be significantly desirable [it] is a more or less powerful (though

40

in no way formal) seism which causes knowledge, or the subject, to vacillate: it creates an emptiness of language (Barthes, 1994, p.4).

The haiku represents a situation in which the linguistically ordinary, everyday, is equivalenced with the syllogistic form in which it is normally subsumed so the meaning of the verse oscillates or trembles as the ordinary, insignificant suffuses the predicates, which in other contexts subsume it, producing a reversal of meaning (ibid., p.71). Here the haiku arguably stands for a wider range of linguistic situations in which the collisions between insignificant everyday meanings and conventional categorisations fuse or connect in a field of associations, rather than the insignificant being routinely subsumed. In this context, the readerly, flat, obvious significations operate against the normal practices of subsumption. As Barthes puts it:

The haiku's task is to achieve exemption from meaning within a perfectly readerly discourse ... readerly, it seems to us simple, close, known ... offered to a whole range of reassuring predicates; insignificant nonetheless, it [the topic] resists us, finally loses the adjectives which a moment before we had bestowed upon it, and enters into that suspension of meaning which ... makes possible the most ordinary exercise of language, which is commentary (ibid., p.81).

Literal[15] (readerly) meaning here dissolves into the meanings it normally suppresses, its trace or ground, raising the possibility of 'commentary', a new perspective), discourse or paradigm. The conditions of predication become manifest as the object itself is revealed as a condition or mediation of predication, thus of foregrounding what lies beyond; the taken for granted, commonplace in such predication. In short, the predicate is seen to be mediated by what it mediates. This subject – predicate reversal can be seen in literary examples where a term is removed from the field of familiar allusions and inserted into a heterogeneous context of associations. This perspectival switch translates the term/object from the ordinary to the extraordinary/exotic in its reference,

---

[15] 'Literalisation' or 'the letter' is used here to interpret 'the readerly' as discourse which suppresses the subject in its context. It does not relate to members of an order of signification in the sense of articulation but appears as natural or 'excessively positive', all-embracing and closed in relation to its content (McNulty, 2012, pp.923, 100, n.10).

signification and so for Barthes it identifies its hidden 'ordinary' content or ground and as such constitutes commentary on its previous status, referential field.

An example given by Žižek (2014, p.157) of the haiku and its enabling of a *tremblé du sens* is as follows:

Old pond.
A frog jumps in
Splash

The breakthrough in perception here is to see 'splash' not as causally related to, or a predication of, 'A frog jumps in' but rather as part of the process of the frog jumping in. In other words, the seism or *tremblé du sens* involves the perception that what is ordinarily taken as a description of what happens is part of the event itself. 'Splash' is assimilated to the frog's movement enabling us to think of this as incorporating the surface disturbance of the pond.

Haiku therefore enables us to see the performative moment of outcomes, that is, as part of a process which they are commonly taken to succeed.[16] The haiku moment so to speak, enables us to overcome the dichotomisation between a process and its product which, as Halewood (2013, p. 159) argues, is characteristic of capitalist modernity. The haiku provides one useful means of capturing the relationality or moment of synthesis hidden behind that of translation as outcome in the shifts from one discursive field (materials, actors, plans etc.) to another (field of product, market etc.).

To complete the account of translation: 'A frog jumps in/Splash' should also be seen as a break with resemblance and routine, that is, with the ordinary. In other words, it marks a moment of differentiation as well as one of synthesis; a point at which new fields reference emerge, are conceptualised.

Translation and Cultural Sociology

Movement between fields of reference or, in du Gay *et al.*'s (1997, pp.15–17) terms, 'Semantic networks' can be seen in more strictly sociological terms if we think of these also as social worlds, that is as fields of discursive practice, interrelation, projects, intentionality and so on. When we move from one social

---

[16] See also Žižek (2014, p.157) for an account of process and break or 'event'.

world or semantic network to another, there is a synthesis or mediation which enables the translation. This is taken for granted in the process of differentiation which consequently takes the previous situation as the ground or link to the new. This hidden resembling function is evident in the usage that relates the new to the originating elements, as du Gay *et al.* (op. cit., p.14) says, by way of illustration of an everyday artefact, the Sony Walkman. When the Walkman was first revealed to the public, a journalist described it as 'a smallish, stereo-headphone cassette player' but

> the…description only works if you already know what such words as 'stereo', 'headphone' and cassette-player mean. What he was really saying was: 'This object works like a small stereo-headphone cassette-player'. He was using words metaphorically.

The writers see these metaphorical translations, as movement between different social worlds which are at the same time semantic networks; individuals exist in networks and these function at once as signifying *and* relational domains, that is, as discursively structured social relations. Here metaphorisation opens up the existing conceptual categories enabling their contents to make new connections, syntheses and in the example we can see this as part of a socio-technological practice.

Similarly, if individuals are moving from one social or semantic world, say, parenting, to that of teaching, they must become less parent-like and more 'teacherly'. They do this by exhibiting the metaphorical trope of resemblance. Thus they use the original resources of family life as a basis for transitioning to the world of teaching: there is both a linking and a differentiation as we, in effect, experience metaphorical transfer from one social world to another. The custodial and instructional values and practices of parenting are re-figured as more formally structured pedagogy, and so on. The importance of resemblance is well recognised as socially necessary. Mauss (2006, p.81) for example, argues that the negotiation of social situations depends on the ability of individuals to imitate models of action they see as prestigious, valued in a particular context, which enables their translation to, acceptance within, that social world.

Translation and Phenomenological Sociology

It has been argued that movement between different discursive fields, a metaphorical transfer, highlights an ontological moment of synthesis in which every day lived experience functions as a means of eliciting connections between discrete materials. This moment can be expressed in terms of phenomenological sociology where we might say that an open horizonal or everyday moment of perception interrupts routine predication revealing the conditions that produce the topic or object and hence how it might be reconfigured. This, in other words, renders visible diverse associations which might facilitate other projects currently inchoate within the current field of reference.

The 'horizon of typical familiarity' (Schutz, 1967, pp.7–8) creates the conditions for such a switch in perspective. Here everything appears as a continuum between the ordinary and the formal systems of thought that are otherwise heterogeneous or differentiated from it as forms of objectified reality. By contrast, lived heterogeneity resides in the situatedness of activity, its reflexive grasp and translations between situated projects, cultural movements, work, urban life etc.

In this horizontal moment, therefore, taken for granted rationalised systems of thought are opened up, so to speak, identifying relations previously hidden; the subscripts signifying the incipience of different projects/trajectories (Schutz, 1970, pp.108–9). In science as in other practices, a shift in contextualisation of a topic or problem, its subscript, occurs and this interrupts and restructures the formal system itself:

> New facts emerge with the shift in the point of view, whereas others that were formerly in the centre of our question disappear... it seems important to me that the scientist keep in mind that each shift in the problem involves a thorough modification of all the concepts and all the types with which he (*sic*) is dealing (ibid., p.109).

The subscripts which situate the objectified systems of thought overlap with these concepts and types themselves. The formal systems are 'already constructed' in terms of the everyday practices of our social worlds. These provide a situatedness or self-referentiality to our identifications (Schutz, 1967, p.6). Morever, the construct is not the same as a fully-fledged classificatory system. Its open horizon of unexplored content suggests it is not a closed (self-identical) conceptual system but a capacity for multiple interpretations. The fact that constructs are not abstractions but wedded to real situations indicates the performative quality of this knowledge (Feather, 2000, p.21).

Schutz's focus on shifts in point of view and in the centrality of particular theoretical problems resonates with themes of translation which have become visible through this chapter. In terms of moving an object or term from one field of reference to another, there is a suppression of some concepts or types but also a continuum or resemblance of the old with the new field. This suggests an identification of relations previously hidden, *sub rosa* in the initial field; a resistance to subsumption, predication which is in other words, an equivocation (*vaciller*) permitting the translation of a term/object from the old field. As Shelley[17] (cited in Burrow, op. cit., p.27) indicates, this involves a kind of semantic or metaphorical transfer which 'marks the before unapprehended relations of things and perpetuates their apprehension...'

Translation as Catachresis

Laclau amongst others has identified catachresis[18] (a significant departure from conventional usage) as the basis of translation. It is the point in the equivalencing of terms at which signification is emptied out, closed. In other words, arguably, the point of equivocation or *vaciller* as captured in Barthes' 'exemption from meaning', which results, in this case, from the juxtaposition of heterogeneous ideas. Laclau sees this trope as instrumental in the construction of hegemony via the idea of articulation as outlined in Gramsci's work (Kraniauskas, 2014, p.31). The present discussion however focuses not on the cultural significance of catachresis, highlighted above, but on the underlying, everyday processes by which this linguistic trope functions. Here it is illuminated by its centrality as a literary characteristic in the poetry of J. H. Prynne which

---

[17] Burrow cites Shelley's *A Defence of Poetry* here.

[18] Laclau (2014) uses catachresis as a 'master trope' in his theorisation of the role of the placeholder in the construction of hegemonic discourse. Metaphorical transfer/translation here differs from the present account in that by emphasising *difference* it merely defers the subject's misrecognition and excludes the possibility that equivocation/*vaciller* may result in a genuine synthesis or apprehension of actuality (Kraniauskas, 2014, pp.31–32).

serves to bring out its more general function in the articulation of the everyday as delineated by Potts in his review of Prynne's work. For example, Potts (2016, p.16) observes regarding the equivocations Prynne uses in one poem 'it is typical that you can't be sure whether the body is a metaphor for the land or vice versa: he keeps both possibilities in suspension'. Again, 'the very moment of focus implies or carries with it a reminder of what is excluded from view' (ibid. p.17). This can, for example, be seen in the lines 'Your tender looks are/frankly incredible' which Potts notes 'packs impressive ambivalence into six superficially romantic words'; a 'confusion of intimacy and calculation' (loc. cit.). As Prynne observes of this experience: 'These moments of contradiction are experienced by the reader initially as immobilising thought in favour of a vehement perplexity, strongly coloured by cross-reference of significance and emotion' (cited in Potts op. cit., p.16). Something of this order can be experienced in the everyday through, for example, the use of sarcasm or *double entendre*, where the listener has to pause – there is an interruption in their train of thought – in order to gather the meaning of the utterance.

Further, as Potts observes, 'Prynne's work persistently evokes interdependence and mutual influence, and the difficulty in grasping it'. The poet works across different fields of reference and it's the jarring collisions between these that provoke insight. *The Oval Window* (referring to the anatomy of the inner ear) is exemplary in this regard:

Filtering and orientation by the human ear is persistently juxtaposed with financial and technological 'windows' onto other data, as well as the literary use of windows and screens. In this way, it intimates what technology and deregulated financial markets might go on to achieve (ibid., p.17).

The violent shifts between semantic fields here force hidden identifications into the open, as the process of translation.

One important conclusion from this discussion of *vaciller* and translation is that subsumption of matters within new fields of discursive practice requires a logically prior process of excavating the resemblance or linkage between objects and concepts or predicates where the process of predication is co-determined by the objects or terms predicated; the moment of the determination of the predicate/subsumptive by its constitutive outside.

The hiding or displacement of this moment is a misrecognition of predication as is evident from Frege who argues that predication is not a process between separate externally related entities; subject and predicate (Carl, 1994, p.67). If we regard predication as an independent function, 'we regard it as having an empty place for the possible designation of an object'. On the contrary, Frege observes, predication has a context, 'a sign never appears without any indication of an object having this property' (Frege, 1979, p.17, cited in Carl, loc. cit.).

As has been suggested throughout this section, the eventuation of a perceptual switch or translation reveals the hidden content of predication as thematic to the new perspective; the existing subject becomes the new predicate, in other words, 'Windows' in Prynne translates from biological features to ways of thinking (predications) about money and communication, for example.

2

Synthesis and Subsumption: The Problem of Unitary Identities in Capitalist Modernity; Case Studies in Sex/Gender and Market Individualisation

Here we move from a consideration of the hidden syntheses in processes of translation to an examination of the problems issuing from the production of identity in formal institutions. The disorientation and misrecognition of individuals, events, products and processes generated by a form of abstraction flowing from the subsumption of lived relations within formal settings will be investigated. Here particular experiences are at one and the same time equivalenced and yet also seen as unique – as vacillating between the one and the other. In modernity, Kant was to indicate this phenomenon in his notion of subreption.

The narrative now turns to Kant who, it is suggested, offers a theoretical underpinning for the idea of a non-unitary identity. This will be employed in the explication of the unitary/non-unitary in the ideologies of binary sex categorisation and individualism. The notion of real abstraction is used to explore the efficacy of these ideologies as discursive practices.

From Barthes to Kant and Subreption: Cross Fertilisation and Misrecognition

While we have concentrated on the transformations that can result from genuine re-articulation/reversal of discursive practices, such as that grounded in Barthes' seism/*vaciller,* we now turn to a writer who at different points saw this equivocation not only as enabling new syntheses or perceptual shifts but, later, also as misrecognition, that is contexts where there is no genuine synthesis, semantic transfer. This might be brought about by subreption (*Erscheichung*); firstly, the idea of the illegitimate transfer of concepts between different bodies of knowledge found in Kant's early 'Dreams of a Spirit Seer' and later, in Kant's *Inaugural Dissertation* prefiguring the Amphiboly of the first *Critique* (Howard, 2014, p.49), the equivalencing of empirical and philosophical concepts. The senses of the two uses of the term overlap[19] and both are relevant to this discussion: the confusion of the sensible with the cognitive, the particular with the general, and earlier, the illegitimate transfer between conceptual or disciplinary domains where a concept disrupts a disciplinary scheme, as with 'woman' and 'biology' (see below).

To elaborate further, these transfers or translations in *The Critique* rely upon a notion of synthesis between the particular and the general which tends to be *sub rosa*, hidden, in the Kant literature itself (ibid., p.50). Its significance is located within Kant's transcendental argument for the unity of experience with the objective world. This flows from a recognition that the links between subjects and predicates, are the same as for concepts and objects, in other words, experience must have an objective basis, thus uniting the world of experiencing individuals and the world that they experience. The argument of the *Critique* is that there is a kind of logical affinity between concepts and objects in the world of cognition and between subjects and predicates in the domain of the sensible (loc. cit.). That is to say, in some sense what is subsumed or classified already contains aspects of what subsumes it. This suggests an inherent hybridity to identities arrived at in this way, what is translated, classified or differentiated also contains similarity with what it subsumes in these identities.

Thus conceptualisation of the experiential is understood as involving a process of synthesis between the outer empirical, sensible world and the inner world of cognition, conceptualisation (the understanding) and takes place in the moment of apperception, which is then, as synthesis of concepts/objects (understanding) and subjects/predicates (sensible world), a necessary condition of cognition, that is, of placing objects under concepts which have empirical content and which, in fact, as such, echoes the arguments around metaphorical transfer/translation in the previous chapter. Kant expresses it as follows:

---

[19] The term or content translated is particular in relation to the generality of the subsuming term or discipline, for instance.

The representation of this unity [synthesis-H.F.] cannot arise out of the combination [of experiences]. On the contrary, it is what, by adding itself to the representation of the manifold[20], first makes possible the concept of the combination (Kant, 1976, p.152).

In the synthesis, the concept is open to its conditions of possibility, is seen as mediated by these and hence as amenable to translation towards these empirical conditions. In other words, the concept appears as in process of formation, translation to an object domain or field of reference by the operations of the understanding.

Subreptive synthesis can be seen as synchronous with the concept's translation in that the understanding represents a moment of translation which co-exists with the field of reference or object domain which the translated concept enters. As such, it is non-identical with itself and provides a counter to the tendencies towards unitary identity, the separation of things, events, and processes from their mediating conditions of possibility. Subreption in the sense used above then pinpoints the process element of identity, as an unfinished or on-going production.

Kant used subreption in this more general sense of metaphoric transfer or moving between different intellectual domains and, as Mensch (2013, cited in Howard op. cit., p.51) indicates, subreption is a central underlying theme of *The Critique*. In this mode of subject-predicate relation, subreption covers inter- or trans-disciplinarity, the cross-fertilisation of conceptual domains. In our context, this may work also from the perspective of everyday life where say, the term 'woman' equivocates cultural and biological significations and any transfer will draw on these. However, for Sandford, it is the critical side of subreption, where there is no genuine translation or synthesis that offers a way forward in addressing ideologies of sex/gender. Sandford (2011, pp.28–9) has argued that the problem of subreption here is that biological abstraction hypostatises lived,

---

[20] 'Manifold' here can be understood as approximating in our terms to a network of connections, cognitive mapping or nascent field of reference. It represents a point of overlap between the cognitive and spatial, sensible worlds, the categorial taken as the logic of empirical entities and relations themselves. See also Merleau-Ponty in Chapter 1 on the spontaneous logic or relationality of things and Barbaras (2004, pp.170–171) on their situated or 'figurative' presentation in Husserl's *hyle;* an 'adumbration (outline-H.F.) of something'.

situated culture, or vice versa: for example, the biological displaces lived cultural experience whilst presenting itself, masquerading as, what in fact is the cultural. Alternatively, constructionist accounts tend to offer a cultural reductionism where the body becomes a blank slate for cultural inscription rather than a figure which offers a physical presence – has posture, gesture, shape and directionality. In either case, following the argument of Chapter 1, the lived experience of the subject is equivalenced to abstract determinants.

Abstractional equivalencing then entails that there is no transfer, articulation of the subject's experience but rather a sleight of hand, misrecognition. In the present case, the lived, plural, doxic qualities of 'woman' that might restrain biological or cultural determinism and on which both depend are lost. The cultural inclusiveness of 'woman' as hetero, lesbian, trans, mother, non-mother etc. on the one side and the assertion of bodily needs on the other are displaced by biological or cultural hypostatisation. In other words, 'woman' is simply obscured by the subsuming abstractions with which, as Sandford (op. cit., p. 29) indicates, there is no synthesis, metaphoric transfer, articulation of the trace but only a confusing cognitive 'shuddering'.

We now turn to examine the oscillation or *vaciller* of meaning in a context which has clear political connotations.

Sandford, 'Woman' and Sex/Gender Equivocation[21]

Sandford (2013, pp.25–6) notes that Beauvoir's use of the term 'woman' unlike many feminist writers, particularly in the Anglophone traditions, where the term represents a point of equivocation in the discourse of heterosexism, does not acknowledge the sex/gender distinction[22]. 'Woman' and 'man' are not philosophical/theoretical categories but are rooted in the doxa of everyday life, as indeed elsewhere Garfinkel (1967) also argues in his discussion of how a transsexual person becomes a woman. 'normal sexuality' as 'the real thing' was

---

[21] In the following discussion, sex has sometimes been placed in inverted commas to emphasise its problematic abstractional usage.

[22] The term '*sexe*' used by Beauvoir; the sense of which also appears in the work of Delphy and Wittig, overlaps sex and gender (Sandford, op cit., pp.26–7). Irigaray's notion of 'sexuate' being also points towards the suppressed complexity of 'sex' (Halewood, op. cit., p. 136).

a serious, situated accomplishment that was produced in concert with others by activities whose prevailing and ordinary success itself subjected their product to Merleau-Ponty's 'préjuge du monde' (ibid., pp.181–2).

This suggests a fundamental ambiguity or instability in the sex/gender distinction. Further, the sex/gender dimensions of the terms 'woman' and 'man' are ideologically functional, as Dorlin (2008) argues, (cited in Sandford, op. cit., p.27) in maintaining a male dominated social regime. If we look at sex as an institutional abstraction ('sex'), then we find that according to medical science, the complex process of sexuation is irreducible to the two categories of sex. Yet the medical management of intersex infants continues to 'support an unambiguous bicategorisation as unquestioned fact'.

Equivocation in the medical discourse of 'sex', for Dorlin as Sandford notes, amounts to a quasi-permanent scientific crisis…because sexual bicategorisation is necessary to reproduce the social relation of dominance that we call 'gender'. Further,

science itself has revealed that sexual bicategorisation is a social and historical norm such that the social relation of 'gender' is in fact the ultimate basis for 'sex' (loc. cit.).

It might also be noted here that according to Laqueur (1990, pp.115, 154ff) categorisation shifted historically between the eighteenth and twentieth-centuries, where biologically, the female was firstly seen as a variant of the male but by the twentieth century had become 'the opposite sex'. In other words, Laqueur is suggesting that the biological is not an entirely separate category from the social, rather that it is permeated by the social: sex and gender shade into each other.

Hence, it can be argued that in modernity the sex/gender discourse of 'sexuate' (sexually diverse; see Halewood, op. cit., p.136) being of the individual operates around an equivocation or crisis of representation where, the doxic format 'woman'/ 'man' cannot be mapped onto the biological dichotomisation of 'sex'. 'Woman' and 'man' occupy the terrain of the sensible; they appear to name the obvious and yet in relation to sex/gender discourse they appear as opaque or resistant to its dualistic interpellations as biological v. cultural being in that 'man/woman' have implications of both biology and culture.

Following the general account of equivocation elaborated by Duroux and others (Hoens, op. cit., pp. 48–9) outlined above, the anchoring of the placeholder or 'letter' in common sense language (doxa) of 'woman' enables the operationalisation of the dualistic 'sex/gender' order of signification. That is, the ambiguity of 'woman' with regard to biological and cultural discourses can be displaced or glossed, thus maintaining the 'logic' of signification in the construction of the social order in terms of 'sex/gender' hierarchies. Nonetheless, 'woman' as suture between biological and cultural discourses remains a weak point in ideological practices of hierarchisation and threatens a *basculer* or *tremblé du sense* as one domain leaks into the other; or to put it another way, when contestation renders the contradictions between significations overt, at this point sense descends into nonsense.

Sandford (op. cit., p.27) notes that the other, non-dualistic side, that is, the wider view of sex ('woman/man' as used above) is pursued in currents of French feminism and that 'sex' as a conceptual object would be 'vacillant' regarding culture and biology; a path that runs through the work of Beauvoir (1972), Delphy (1991, 1993) and Wittig (1992). These writers can be seen as mobilising the categories 'woman', 'man' or '*sexe*' as terms which can displace sex/gender by refusing the culture-biology dualism and its oppressive ideological consequence: 'biology as destiny'.

Elsewhere the vacillant nature of this dualism is evident when we consider the 'biological' body in existential phenomenology (Merleau-Ponty, 1992b, pp.248–51) where the body as lived body exists in relation to a process of embodiment. Here the physical body is coterminous with its environment and practices; the body is always already discursive as a 'figure'. This is seen via the phenomenon of body language and the related notions of posture and gesture which reveal the intrinsically intentional nature of the body, its imbrication with meaning, and orientation to its surroundings (Giddens, p.65). The embodied or lived body is the way the body experiences itself, is experienced by the individual and as such provides a critical reference point against the ways in which it is identified in forms of hierarchical classification, those of medical science and other official discourses which serve to regulate identities. This latter culturally dominant tendency is pinpointed by Foucault (1984, p.154) in his critique of sex/gender in his well-known statement that sex is constituted as a 'fictitious unity', of different institutional discursive practices.

As Sandford (op. cit., p.26) notes, 'sex' is a modern concept in its binary form where sexual identities are seen as contained in individuals rather than the overlapping sexuate beings entertained by Irigaray (1985) where sex appears as a mutually permeable 'duality' (Halewood op. cit., p.135). Here sex is 'more than one', that is, not a unitary entity but a result of the hybridisation of polar positions. It is however, this unitary view that Sandford sees as operating in a functionally regulative way in modern societies.

Following a quasi-Kantian argument, Sandford (op. cit., p.28) suggests that due to its role as a regulative or functional idea in a society dominated by men, sex as described above becomes, in effect, a real category or 'object in the idea', an equivocation between abstract and concrete things. As such 'sex' manifests itself both in concrete instances (bodily appearance, for instance) and in more abstract forms, individuals classified by sex in the sphere of institutional identifications and the two are confused or conflated in the everyday experience of 'sex'. In this equivocation, sex as an abstraction becomes a kind of object by default. Consequently, the question arises as to how such a 'transcendental illusion' can be maintained.

As with the discussion of Barthes and haiku, Sandford (op. cit., p.29) suggests that equivocation occurs where the ordinary, situated or lived utterances are equivalenced with the more abstract usages, giving 'sex' a more object-like character. In the case of male hegemony in the sexual order, the equivocation is resolved by hypostatisation – naturalisation or reification of the abstraction. Concrete, ordinary manifestations of 'sex' are misrecognised via abstract binary categories. There is a confusion of one with the other in a perceptual sleight of hand. Further, it can be suggested that because this naturalisation of 'sex' entails that sex is sutured as contained within individual bodies and not a hybrid, synthetic and relational process, its signification can't be based on lived experience of its hybridity. Rather it is based on the imposition of bicategorisation onto diverse and hybrid experiences. This represents a fragmentation of discursive relations between agents, unable to identify and communicate their *de facto* common experiences, a disjunction between experience and classification systems. The consequence of bicategorisation is a series of gaps or silences in relational processes; a 'conceptual juddering' (loc. cit.) or point of incipient failure in the signifying order. In this case, the discursive impact of medical science is to disarticulate the term 'woman' from its lived discursive context and present it in the vacillant form as both concrete and abstract, where it creates the ideological effects of immediacy, individual sexual identity as universal biological fact. The institutional politics of 'sex' is writ large here.

However, where relations of domination are challenged situationally, the concreteness of context, its haecceity, offers a way beyond reification by means of new situational definitions of woman such that 'working woman', whatever its negative gender connotations translates women into a new context contesting the traditional meaning of 'woman'. In other words, equivocation doesn't have to end in reification and misrecognition but can bring a perceptual switch, as indicated in Duroux and Barthes above.

It's at this weak point then that the signifying order breaks down as cultural/biological dualism fails to articulate what it is to be a woman; the equivalencing of sex as a binary abstraction with its more concrete, lived manifestations is interrupted, as this gap in signification represented by 'woman' becomes productive as an opening onto a new field of reference, that of the working woman. Another way of describing this process is as one of contestation and translation in a way that transcends this reification of being (culturally) defined by 'biology'.

Discussions about genetic determination of sex/gender have incidentally also faltered over the cultural and biological duality in the case of LGBT+ identities (arguably forms of subreptive cross-fertilisation[23]) where cultural properties have been identified with biological entities, the 'gay gene', for example, ironically making the problematicity of sex/gender more evident. In line with this, Derrida for example, has argued, the categories 'nature' and 'culture' tend to leak into each other and the positivity of each is due to its hidden synthesis with and reinforcement by its opposite! According to dualism, biology should be self-sufficient as a description and explanation of a certain conduct and yet it needs supplementing by a cultural description. Derrida (1982, p.145) in effect describes a subreptive confusion where biological (natural) positivity needs supplementing by culture.

---

[23] The moment of hybridisation or synthesis is often displaced, hidden here and identities appear as self-contained entities, which is one of the criticisms levelled at identity politics; one sees the product identity but not the process that is intertwined with this outcome which although hidden continues to sustain it as an underlying hybridity, a more than unitary self.

Each of the two significations (nature and culture-H.F.) is by turns effaced or becomes discreetly vague in the presence of the other. But their common function is shown in this: whether it adds or substitutes itself, the supplement is exterior, outside of the positivity to which it is super-added, alien to that, which in order to be replaced by it must be other than it.

Therefore, 'if it fills, it is as if one fills a void', it produces no relief (loc. cit.). The subreptive dualisms of sex/gender identified by Sandford are arguably illuminated by Derrida's account of supplementation here, especially in regard to the anxiety, alienation or lack of relief produced for those subjected to or interpellated by discourses of 'naturalisation' which through a politics of sex displaces any biology/culture hybridisation and in doing so prevents the individual from relating their sex to their cultural situation. Further, Derrida (loc. cit.) demonstrates the incoherence that follows from not allowing a mutual permeability of culture and nature. If these terms/entities are indeed self-sufficient, then this is represented in the order of signification by 'The mark of an emptiness'…the supplement is the place where signification breaks down.

In other words, the more one elaborates on the nature of the 'gay gene', for example, that is, describes what biology does, the more one draws on cultural factors such as conduct to fill the gap in the biological explanation[24]. It is likewise with the attempts to define biological sex in the case of women via marriage, mothering, bodily comportment, for example. All have biological elements but that is not the full story as cultural variation in conduct shows.

As Sandford concludes, sex/gender functions politically, it has real effects. The question remains as to whether 'sex' as a modern idea can also be a kind of real abstraction, functioning institutionally in a Foucauldian manner as a set of discursive practices to maintain a hierarchy between men and women by equivalencing all bodies designated as male as against all those termed female; whether in modernity the lived sexuality of agents is subsumed under abstract institutional-political requirements, and people are consequently confronted with their sexuality as an externality. Finally, if this is the case, are hierarchies a result of colonisation of a politics of sex in everyday interactions, ordinary accounts and deployments of sex does science here, as Dorlin (see above) suggests, base itself, on the doxa of sex, that is, on institutionalisation or formalisation of the

---

[24] See also Meehan Crist's comments on 'race' and biology in the following section.

everyday significations of lived sexuality? Is the abstraction 'sex' therefore ontologically derivative, a 'colonisation' of its everyday usage?

We can at least relate a politics of 'sex' as male domination to the theme of subreption highlighted by Sandford. The vacillation between culturally mediated concrete experience of sex and its abstract biological definition is productive, as Sandford (op. cit., p.27) suggests and the present author takes the idea forward by viewing the 'conceptual juddering' as a displacement where one thing is signified by another where the abstraction gains its life or being from the concrete, lived side of the equivocation. Hence the abstraction, a reworking of Sandford's Kantian regulative idea, is a derivative but none the less real form of being. Arthur's (2001) treatment of capital and abstract labour as formal or abstract being in relation to living, concrete labour is arguably a useful parallel here (see below). In Chapter 3, it is suggested the representational aspect is key in that abstraction is seen to feed off the lived existence and appears in its guise. More generally, the metaphors of duplicity, the uncanny, *Unheimliche*, spectrality or hauntology (Derrida) suggest a hidden, suppressed/subsumed content that operationalises, dynamises the semblances which displace it.

The stereotype 'woman' indicates amongst other things that the diversity, polysemy and haeccity, concreteness of situation, is obscured and represented in a readerly, literal form which therefore hides its contextual specificities, that is, polysemic potential. As Sandford's argument suggests, the notion of 'woman' is crucial to the sex/gender equivocation. In other words, the doxic of the everyday has a function as an indexical marker or trace against which we elaborate situational identities and it is through this doxic content that institutionally-based hypostatised classificatory hierarchies of the social relations of 'sex' can be contested.

The objective historical illusion of sex is…the transcendental subreption of this relation…the effective reification of the concept, at the highest level of generality, empirically instantiated in almost every aspect of our lives. Avoiding [this]…subreption [although involving] theoretical vigilance…is a political struggle at the level of everyday experience. The question of the meaning of sex is not a dispute to be settled by intellectuals or scholars; it is the lived contradiction of our sexed existence today (ibid., p.29).

And, more generally, the suppressed situating features of unitary identity (the 'non-identical'), it is argued here, provide a background framework or referential field through which new translations and subjects emerge.

Unitary Identities: Reflections on General Issues

The abstractional nature of the dominant culture of modern capitalist societies has been evidenced in the discussion of sex/gender. Whilst the categories of sex/gender, nature/culture, material/social are often abstracted from everyday life as representing distinct ontological realms it has been argue that this is fictive. The binaries here rely on each other; one forms the background to the other and neither can be seen as a unitary identity of an entity. For example, as Crist has argued in the case of 'race' and genetic reductionism and which can equally apply to, for example, sex and gender, every genetic argument about 'race' requires a cultural narrative, a story of 'race' in this case; or in our context, a story of 'sex' is the focus. Hence, as Crist (2018, p.4) argues, objections to biological reductionist accounts of identity here are not based on mistakes about whether X is a biological or cultural fact but on an 'error' which is 'one of logic', the inextricably socio-cultural situatedness of 'biological facts'.

> You can't look to genes for a story of race if you don't already have a story of race in mind. (loc. cit.)

This links to our previous discussion of Frege on the subject-predicate relation and his critique of the prevailing sense that subject and predicate, the object and its concept are treated syntactically rather than performatively. They therefore appear as autonomous entities, universal rather than situated, codetermining each other, and are seen as only subsequently brought into relation, equivalenced (Carl, op. cit., p. 67). Frege, however, noted that

> a sign for a property [predicate-H.F.] never appears without any indication of an object having the property (Frege, 1979, p.17).

In other words, the property or predicate is always codetermined, situated by its object. Further, as Carl argues in support of this view

The traditional [subject-predicate-H.F.] view does not give any hint about the real nature of concepts, because the notion of predicate does not entail the idea that concepts are 'unsaturated' (op. cit., pp.67–8).

That is, it doesn't take into account the idea that concepts are not closed, self-contained entities and that they are open to their grounds, situation, conditions of possibility, situated classifications indicated by their object. Hence the effect of subject-predicate equivalencing is to suggest that the predicate exhausts the meaning of its subject: it is autonomous, rather than situationally specific, and therefore, generally applicable, and so wholly contains the particularity of its topic. The latter then appears via the equivalencing as both concrete and general. This indicates the experience of *vaciller* noted by Sandford in her discussion of ideologies of 'sex', an overwhelming sense of compulsion to accept 'sex' as the truth of 'woman' (and 'man') which is at the same time a gap or hiatus in the abstractional discourse of sex/gender and the possibility that it may be challenged.

Abstractional discourse operates in an antinomial fashion. If the claim was made that Y is biological, then because Y is equivalenced with biology, no cultural predication is necessary, 'biological' is essentially what Y is, to the exclusion of cultural predicates. This is because the predicate here operates as an abstraction in the manner discussed above where 'sex' appears in a biological guise that explains all forms of gendered conduct, that is, explains what 'woman' means. It is universal and concrete.

This synopsis of 'sex' as abstraction echoes Hegel's description of the equivalencing role of money in Chapter1. Here services are equivalenced by an external mediator, money. Money is a universalising form of equivalencing. In terms of the services, it equivalences them, produces them ontologically as real abstractions, that is, as the same. Hence with 'sex', biology becomes an abstraction, as does culture, and as such these categories are mutually exclusive, external to each other (via the mediation of 'sex'). The paradoxical nature of such mediation is that although mutually exclusive, the categories are essentially the same, as 'sex' reduces whichever term it colonises to the discursively dominant abstraction, in this case, the predicate 'biological'.

However, the path we've taken in criticising abstraction leads us to suggest that such antinomialism is mistaken, that 'sex' may have, for example, both biological and cultural predicates. As Halewood, in line with the excursus on

Hegel above, has argued in relation to sex/gender exclusions from definitions such as those of 'man' or 'woman' that they are often based on this abstractional and oppositional form of non-inclusion.

> In this way, being is defined in terms of opposition. 'what is a man?' "Well, whatever a man is, he is certainly not a woman." The so-called evidence to back up such claims is then premised on that which is specific to that sex, and not to the other. Whether this is done in terms of genitalia, hormones, chromosomes, the presumption is the same; identity proceeds from opposition, not from similarity or relationality (Halewood, op. cit., p.138).

Hence to see subject and predicate as separate is to omit the process element, the relationality of co-determination, the synthesis between the terms, between the concept and predicating experience or 'story' that is needed to produce a translation of an entity into a different field of reference, biology, culture or whatever, and that this leaves a trace or context, a subscript to the newly defined entity which marks out its ground, its conditions of possibility.

A concept closer to home, everyday life, tends to produce the opposite form of antinomialism; a cultural assimilation of a fundamentally polymorphous term. 'Everyday' and even 'life' but especially when conjoined, produce an overwhelmingly cultural association, connotative effect. There is a translation or synthesis which depends on difference to evoke similarities but this is effaced by homogenisation of 'life' with 'everyday'. As pointed out in the case of catachresis above, strong elements of difference can produce effective translation as with 'snowball in hell's chance'. The biological connotations of 'life' however are lost in its assimilation to 'everyday' and the metaphorical tensions displaced as 'dead' or 'worn away' metaphor, a state of affairs which reduces the capacity for linguistic reflexivity, a point which applies across the board. Under these circumstances, colonisation by formal institutions, as in Dorlin's account of 'sex' is more likely.[25]

Identity and hybridisation

The alternative outcome from abstractional *vaciller* in Kant's comments on subreption, as Howard (2014, p.49) suggests is a genuine synthesis or

---

[25] See Derrida (1974) on *usure* and 'worn away' metaphor.

articulation where a concept is translated between different fields of reference thus achieving new identifications. As argued above, the sense of difference in this process is often accentuated at the expense of the synthesis which enables this translation to take place; the synthesis or process element of translation is lost, displaced, *sub rosa* as Howard (op. cit., p.51) noted for instance in relation to Kant scholarship.

This hybridisation is another way of looking at the incompleteness of identity, the sense that whatever one is dependent on some translation which involves the incorporation of something suppressed within that form of recognition, as the metaphorical model of translation suggests (Waldron, op. cit., p.167) and which may be open to revivification if situation prompts.

An illustration of the problematic treatment of hybridity is the tendency to suggest that identities exist in a state of completeness and are then, as externalities mixed, fused etc. rather than being situationally prompted because of what they already commonly contain in an unarticulated form – 'suppressed associations' as Waldron's model of metaphorical translation suggests (loc. cit.). As Halewood's (op. cit., pp.162–3) work makes clear, translation or process co-exists with its outcomes/abstractions and hence the actuality of identity is that it continues to be mediated by its translation or moment of synthesis. In this moment, entities are biological etc. in the sense of being 'biology-like', rather than being exhaustively biological. The idea of metaphorical translation as ongoing mediator and critique of identities is taken up again in Ch 4.

Globalisation theory might be an example of identities seen as externalities where 'global' and 'local' are conceived of as in different boxes and then brought together as a globalisation of a (passive) 'local', rather than the two as part of a relational process dependent on active internal constituents of the two moments of globalisation. In terms of music, Ska, Reggae, Rap and Grime in the U.K. for example, begin with a limited constituency, but this broadens out and speaks to a far wider audience who are capable of identifying the sound with what they already 'know', the 'global' of the subject's horizonal context.

To return to the sphere of sex/gender, Halewood's (op. cit., p.136) identification, following Irigaray on this point, of hybridity in terms of 'sexuate' being and the failure to map sex/gender binary abstractions ('sex') onto individual bodies results, as Sandford has argued, in *vaciller,* where the abstraction fails to represent the lived experience of particular women (and men). This equivocation or hiatus is a space in which 'sex', as it encounters the everyday might be reappropriated as Sandford also suggests; a synthesis in which bicategorisation is the recuperated raw material of more plural identifications. Here, following the Duroux/Miller interpretation of suture in Chapter 1, 'sex' can be seen as a placeholder or suture, the site of the repression of subjectivity in gendered discourse but also the place where the subject might through contestation rearticulate and express their desire through a shift or translation of lived identity to a different signifying order.

The Spirit of Modern Capitalism: Abstraction from Weber to Derrida

From what has been argued above, it can be seen that (a) conceptions of the biological and the cultural cannot, in actuality be entirely disentangled; and (b) that there is a confusion of particular and general cases which results from the abstract equivalencing, that is, subsumption of, lived relations. Consequent upon this abstractional equivalencing is the treatment of the individual as separate from the generality of socio-cultural context.

It has been shown that sexual typifications or categories cannot be mapped onto individual bodies in an unproblematic way, that is, there is no necessary one-to-one fit between bodies and 'sex' in the sense in which this term has been used here. Bodies can possess 'sex' in various hybridised forms. This is, it is suggested, one specific case of a more general argument about identities and their 'distributed' or relational/overlapping nature. However, as Halewood (op. cit., p.137) argues, modern capitalist societies tend to fix identities within individuals as we've seen with sexual bicategorisation. In the case of 'sex' (or 'woman'), the 'biological individual' reinforces the ideas of a self-contained individual or *homo clausus* as a natural entity and as a result social-gender roles appear as natural, imbricated within this 'biological' individual.

The work of Elias (2000, pp.471–482) as developed by du Gay (2008, p.27ff) and others (notably Callon and Latour) seeks to show how identities or personas emerge from wider networks or 'figurations'. Elias offers an account of how modern capitalism figures individuals as autonomous or externally related beings[26], that is, produces socially, something that looks like the opposite of a social existence. This individual – social contrast is in some ways similar to the

[26] Hence the individual paradoxically appears both as a particularity and as absolutised-universal; the 'free individual' both includes and excludes everything else.

argument about the cultural and the biological ('nature') as mutually exclusive categories, as seen in the sex/gender discussion above. Elias locates this reification of the individual in his concept of *homo clausus* which is a generic case of *homo economicus* etc. where the individual and the social appear as two separate entities and then interact[27]. The social process as dynamic in the formation of individuals is displaced, producing a false or 'misplaced concreteness' (Halewood, op. cit., p.159). As suggested, Elias counterposes the idea of figuration to this. However, as du Gay (2008, p. 30) argues, in an echo of the discussion of sex bicategorisation, for Elias the *homo clausus* is in some sense none the less real.

du Gay (op. cit. p.47) notes that the idea of selfhood or persona as contained within the individual developed in early modern Europe based on two kinds of formal institutional practices. Firstly, legal rights and obligations drew on the Roman legal code which enshrined rights in a free individual or citizen. Obligations were framed as essentially between individuals rather than individuals and social groups.

Contractual relations became increasingly important in early modern Britain where differentiation in the division of labour led to increased interdependency, networks or figurations of individuals, as Elias (op cit., pp. 481–3) argues. This sense of the individual person involved the internalisations of norms of conduct and growth of self-regulation; an obligated or contracted personage.

The second key factor in the instantiation of the *homo clausus* was identified by Weber as the development of Puritan religious institutional practices promoting right conduct as a sign of individual salvation. Importantly, as Weber went on to adduce there was an elective affinity between this kind of person and the practice of capital accumulation which involved the interpellation of subjects as individuals via the market. As du Gay (op. cit., p. 48) notes

Weber explores the way in which modern forms of economic conduct, the rigorous organisation of work, a distinctively methodical approach to labour, a systematic pursuit of profit, developed out of the religious practices of the sixteenth- and seventeenth-century Puritan sect.

---

[27] See, for instance, the individual-social dichotomies in the work of Weber and Durkheim (Feather 2010, pp.42, 44ff).

However, some qualifications need to be made regarding the ascendancy of the *homo clausus* persona, as Elias's account of figurations and interdependency indicates, because Elias distinguishes the figuration with its life-world type reciprocal agreements between networked individuals from the economic agent constructed within these early modern institutional arrangements.

As noted above, Elias's account suggests that the institutional practices were internalised as a form of self-regulation. These were then paradoxically experienced at one and the same time both as part of the agent's own motivations and as an external compulsion…pointing towards the complexity of individualised agency. This equivocation and the anxieties flowing from it might go some way to explaining the 'spirit' or powerful motivating force behind capitalist accumulation practices.

Now du Gay's focus is that the norms of conduct are internalised and the experience of their externality drops out of the discussion. It is however necessary to stress that internalisation cannot take place without the discursive practices of Puritanism and capital accumulation which reproduce the processes of internalisation. Further, there has to be a substrate for these abstractional practices to work on, namely the concrete individual. In du Gay's account, individual and persona merge in a constructionist reading of the *homo clausus*.

This ignores the fact that as Weber (cited in du Gay, pp.48–9) and Sukov, 2009 (cited in Leiberknecht et al. 2019)[28] *inter alia*, have suggested, the concrete individual also experiences the abstractional practices of the *homo clausus* as an external compulsion (God's providential will as well as methodical self-regulation). Sukov (loc. cit.) is seen to note on Elias's self-regulating individual that

> the internalised external compulsion is experienced as the limitation and separation of the self because it increasingly prevents the individual from living out his (*sic*) spontaneous affects [hence it is seen as] limiting from the outside.

---

[28] The citation (Leiberknecht et al., 2019) which follows appears to be a précis of Sukov's argument on Elias's self-regulating individual. It in any case offers a neat encapsulation of the tensions derived from the internal and external aspects of the way the *homo clausus* is experienced.

Indeed, this sense of external direction, or alienated self, recalls Hegel's observation (see Chapter 1) that the economic /legal equivalencing of concrete roles, dispositions, services, talents and so on appears as an extreme externality, indeed as a 'thing' but something which is none the less a necessary part of establishing equity in the modern world. As such, abstraction displaces the experiential, situated nature of their use value.

In du Gay's case, the idea that personas are internalised is insufficient to describe the *homo clausus* abstraction. As Sukov argued, the subject experiences the persona as an external power. This *vaciller* between internal and external then explains the compulsion of the abstraction as simultaneously one's own motivation and an external force, that of the world of institutional power and legitimacy. There is then a clear parallel with the effects on the individual of Protestantism as at once self-driven and subject to external providential intervention. The indeterminacy of abstractional *vaciller* between the two poles dynamises the individual who is thereby driven by their uncertainty and consequent salvation anxiety. The fact that the abstraction is experienced as a compelling externality drops out of du Gay's discussion and there is consequently no objective basis here for the way the internalised protestant persona is experienced.

It's also clear from Hegel's account of abstraction that the thingness of abstractions is not an illusion or misrecognition of contract, money, property relations, and the market, and so on but rather instead the kinds of abstractions discussed here are substantial mediations of modernity.

It can be concluded that the internal/external 'paradox' is demonstrably an example of *vaciller* where abstractional subsumption of concrete services etc. maintains the indeterminacy of reference, the conceptual juddering referred to by Sandford. The compulsions driving individual conduct seem both immediate, that is, internal and yet are also experienced as an external and so impersonal/universal influence. Hence arguably as institutional abstractions they colonise the lived experience and reciprocity of say, figurational obligations rendering them absolute rather than negotiable. However, the countervailing influences of lifeworld group reciprocities might indicate a negotiable route through institutional life as Strauss (1964) has argued, via a 'negotiated order'.

The above discussion reinforces Halewood's (op. cit., pp.159–60) use of Marx to suggest that the monadic *homo clausus* is something that emerges as an abstraction from modern capitalism where the state and the labour market jointly produce 'the individual'. On the one side the state, via individual rights, citizenship, guarantees the free movement of labour, legitimising the labour market, which has from its side effectively abolished traditional ties to the land. The ramifications of the *homo clausus* can be felt in social theory as du Gay (2008, p.31) argues. The dualisms between agency and structure, micro and macro sociology suggest a suture or void, a point of equivocation in the signifying order of social enquiry. Giddens' (2001) critique of sociological dualism and attempt to move beyond this highlights the individual as a problematic abstraction in modern social theory. This sociological dualism is arguably an instance of wider ideological formations around the *homo clausus*. To use Sandford's (op. cit., p.29) approach here we can see that the individual appears as both concrete, living being and as an abstraction, and that the former is displaced ideologically by the latter, as Halewood's references above to Marx suggest, where the institutionally subsumed individual appears jointly as a market abstraction and also as a state-bureaucratic abstraction, the citoyen. The actual, lived existence of the individual there appears as equivalenced ideologically to these abstractions although, as Sandford's approach suggests, we can see this is not accomplished without some 'conceptual juddering'.

Vis á vis ideology there is a commonality between Sandford and Marx in that firstly, in both cases something concrete, be it sex/woman as lived reality or labour as living labour are respectively subsumed under 'woman/sex' as a general category and living labour as abstract labour. Secondly, the idea of woman/sex and of abstract labour is taken for the actual lived reality. In formal institutional discourse, 'woman', as Dorlin has argued, is a bureaucratic-scientistic abstraction and this appears as incarnated in actual women, fixing them biologically (Sandford, op. cit., p.27). Again, vis á vis the economic individual, actual labour power translated economistically as 'labour' takes on the ghostly compulsion of the market price. In both cases, there is an equivocation or incoherence between concrete and abstract registers such that 'woman' and 'labour', ideologically speaking, represent weak points or a suture in signifying practices.

In the context of the suture (see Miller and Duroux in Chapter 1), these terms represent 'the literal', they are placeholders through which the logic of a discourse is operationalised. In the case of abstractional subsumption, as argued above, there is a *vaciller*, an on-going failure to interpellate human beings as subjects. This represents a crisis of signification around say, the historically determinate ambiguities, contradictions of 'woman' or 'labour' and is indicative of a reflexive moment where, as Sandford's discussion of 'sex' suggests the subject might break out through accessing the doxa of 'the literal' in a different way, that is, through the experience of contestation and thus be translated to a new field of reference. (This theme will be pursued more empirically in Chapter 3).

Vaciller where there can be no synthesis and translation, that is, where there is no articulation of a lived content can also be illustrated by returning to Marx where we can bring out the issues of doubleness, spectrality and displacement around abstraction and ideology. Commodification, as transforming concrete existents, renders them as abstractions but in the sense that they appear as possessed by the spirit or spectre of capital. Their 'reality' is thus displaced by this spectrality such that they appear as the 'sensuous supersensuous', to use one of Marx's (1976, p.165) descriptions of the apprehension of the commodification process. There is an equivocation here between the generality of capital and the sensuous particularity of concrete things such that the concrete appears both as unique and also in its spectral mode, as universal. An exploration of Marx's work reveals an ontological argument about this form of displacement as the work of Arthur (2001) shows.

Arthur's work on the spectrality of capital offers a way of grasping the ontology of abstraction, the real abstraction predicated on exchange relations and its impact on its subjects (ibid., 2001, p.33). He asks whether Marx's use of the terminology of spectrality is just incidental to his account of the subsumption or abstraction of living labour under capitalism, or refers to something 'much more than rhetoric'; that is, a descriptive level which has referential import for an ontology of capital. The genesis of value in production, it is argued, is clearly dependent on a concrete substratum of labour in the following manner.

> Value is a shape opposed to all materiality, a form without content, which yet takes possession of our [lived – H.F.] world in the only way it can, through draining it of reality, an ontological vampire that bloats its hollow form at our expense (ibid., p.39)

The ghostly nature of abstraction/subsumption is further adumbrated in the description of life under capitalism as a doubleness: 'all is *always* 'another thing' than what it is' (loc. cit.). As already noted, Marx has described this form of experience as the 'sensuous supersensuousness' (ibid., p.32), the equivalencing of universal/abstractional and concrete modes of existence where the concrete, as inhabited by the spirit of capitalism, is always more than itself.

Similarly, Arthur (op. cit., p.39) notes, Derrida has argued that the spirit, idea or trajectory of capital is unlike that of other intentionalities in that these achieve some concrete realisations, embodiment whilst the spectre of value has no concrete equivalent or haecceity.[29] On the contrary, it equivalences or abstracts concrete realities via its money form (Derrida cited ibid., p.39). It thus, arguably, effects a double equivalence: an equivocation between concrete entities as a result of the equivocation between concrete entities and their abstractions as commodities.

Capital is thus always the being beyond itself: in its 'spectral phenomenology' all commodities appear as 'its avatars, an uncanny identity of discernibles' (loc. cit.). This 'concrete-abstract' equivocation expresses a void, the non-being of capital. As Arthur notes,

> There is a void at the heart of capitalism. It arises because of the nature of commodity exchange, which abstracts from, or absents, the entire substance of use value. This originary displacement of the material process of production and circulation by the ghostly objectivity of value is supplemented when the spectre of capital takes possession of it. (Arthur, 2001, p.32).

Some commonalities can be seen to exist between the operationalisation of the discursive/signifying practice of capital as value creation via subsumption of concrete life, and the bureaucratic structures of modernity. The latter echoes capital in its focus on legal-contractual rationality and the interpellation of the

---

[29] Derrida (1994, p.127) makes the broader point that in modern capitalism institutional structures are living abstractions, 'formal bod(ies)' not merely idealisations in the Weberian mode but the appearance of these as real. '...the fetish would be given or rather lent, a borrowed body, the second incarnation conferred on an initial idealisation, the incorporation in a body that is...neither perceptible nor invisible but remains flesh, in a body without nature...a technical body or an institutional body.' This challenges the presupposition that institutions have a fundamental substantiality as found in say, dualistic social theory. He does not investigate whether the ontology of capitalist modernity renders 'formal bodies' as both abstract and real – real abstractions.

individual as a legal entity tied into states via citizenship: this is the other legitimation side of Elias's *homo clausus*; the economic and the legal individual are two sides of the same coin. This parallelism leads us to infer that there is a mutuality or elective affinity between the structures of capitalism and modernity in its Weberian sense.

The latter is effectively illustrated by Foucault (1999, p.102) in his account of the way formal institutions instigate programmes of discipline or training which involves the subjectification of concrete individuals through techniques where discipline

> measures in quantitative terms and hierarchises in terms of value the abilities, the level, the 'nature' of individuals compares, differentiates, hierarchises, homogenises, excludes. In short, it normalises.

Here the equivalencing processes of abstraction familiar to capitalism can be seen at work but although, as Foucault (loc. cit.) points out, formal institutions are characterised by legal-rational relations that is not what dynamises them or renders them functional. It is, rather the application of a norm (see above) that serves to operationalise or give direction to these abstract relations or structures. In other words, the abstractions of capitalist modernity require a colonisation of the culture of everyday life, the routines through which it functions, although the distinction between equivalence and its operationalisation, how it is measured, is not made by Foucault himself.

Hence this insight into the nature of bureaucracy and its need for external operationalisation, 'repair work' from interactional life, which as Cuff, Sharrock et al. (1992, pp.176–179) imply[30], supports the view that bureaucracy is ontologically derivative. Habermas (1999, p.183) has also argued for the secondary nature of 'system' to life-world, in this case via the latter's 'colonisation' by the system world. In this manner, 'systemic mechanisms' suppress aspects of the life-world ('forms of social integration') that the system itself ultimately depends on. It is suggested here though that system and life-

---

[30] Their work is adapted here in the very specific sense that there is a distinction between how people do things and the institutional framework within which it is done; 'repair work' means both how formal institutional aims are operationalised and the accounts given of this interpretation of formal, explicit rules and procedures.

world are not separate and autonomous[31] but rather intertwined entities[32] and this leads to a 'hauntology' of misrecognition. As such, the abstraction substitutes for the goals of concrete life, whether as 'value' in capital or as instrumental rationality in the case of other formal organisations. In both cases, these mediations of social life come to dominate, displace concrete life itself. This turns mediational processes into things, a false or misplaced concreteness (Halewood, op. cit., p.159) which externalises the individual in/against their relational existence. Ultimately, what is displaced, in both cases, as Habermas (loc. cit.) intimates, is the fundamental democratic, peer-based relations of everyday life and its communicative potential, its 'consensus-dependent coordination of action'.

This, as structuralists and phenomenologists have suggested in their different ways, is what gets colonised as the 'readerly'/reified discursivity of capitalist modernity. The displacement of non-hierarchical sensibility entails the suppression of the plurivocity of discourse, its interactional moment. The peculiar nature of the 'system' element of modernity is evident in the effect of doubleness; the confusion or equivocation between abstraction of concrete life and concrete life itself. However, the doxic nature of lived experience is not only elided with but can also be an interruption of the ideological discourse where the latter comes to appear meaningless, absurd and, given a politics of situation, the lived trace or subscript can be reappropriated and shifted to a new field of reference. The value of work as use value versus market value, or the reciprocity of organisation members versus management, sponsored 'teamwork' (see Chapter 5), highlight points at which signification judders, vacillates, in Barthes' terms a seism or *tremblé du sens*.

---

[31] Habermas's (1999) dualistic account of the social world is epitomised in his counterposing of interactional life and a functionalist systems approach which reproduces the conundrums of the agency-structure dichotomy in classical social theory.
[32] The system element is seen as both operationalised and critiqued in everyday life.

3

The 'Meaninglessness' of
Hegemonic Crises

This chapter argues in a programmatic way that hegemonic crises involve subjects being unable to pick out/identify new realities; that this is symptomatic of emergent historical trends and creates a crisis of meaning from the level of individual projects to 'intentional history' itself. This gives rise to somatic effects that is, existential insecurity, anxiety, disorientation, demotivation etc., or in Merleau-Ponty's terms, a sense of 'terror' in the face of historical events. The somatics of insecurity are experienced both by those in dominant and subaltern positions as unsuccessful substitution or displacement of failing institutional projects; that is, rearticulation within the discursive or ideological conjuncture is no longer an effective strategy. Hence under such a crisis of articulation or discursive hiatus the various emancipatory trends of the time may cease to sustain what have become patently vicarious routes or digressions.

As argued in Chapter 2, it is not that as with Barthes, there is a seism, a void in meaning which results in a translation of lived experience to a new field of reference but rather that the subject has been colonised by abstractions which have no articulation with the lived world as they possess no specific content, 'a form without content', an 'empty universal' as Arthur (op. cit., pp.39, 41) argues regarding money as a mediator of needs. Rather such placeholders mimic or haunt an articulation of lived experience. Such a mediation constitutes a placeholder in discourse that functions not just by displacing elements of situated life and their contradictions but by equivalencing terms without regard to their discursive content.

As Arthur (2001, p.41) suggests vis a vis exchange relations within modern capitalism, two different ontologies are linked, but they are nothing to each other: each is something and as such capable of acting but to the other it is nothing, non-being.[33] Hence a *vaciller* obtains between these realms of abstraction and concrete being but as with Sandford's 'object in the idea' where sex is alternatively a lived relation and an abstract category there is a *pas de deux*, a mimicry or shadowing which can never be a union or articulation because these are different domains of being, one of which, as with money, arbitrarily equivalences the concrete use values of the other.

The desuetude of historical projects can be understood in these terms, that is, as a crisis of signification; they become meaningless as they no longer have a purchase on everyday life. Under these conditions things appear as arbitrarily equivalenced. That is, as equivalenced by an external force rather than by an intrinsic congruence or mutual affinity. This sense of separateness, externality of, or to, one's experiences, is then the concomitant of the discursive void that is abstract equivalencing.

As intimated, the hiatus in historical discursive practice is redolent of Hegel and Marx's view of money where living labour is equivalenced via market and contract, an 'extreme externality' (Hegel). Under these conditions the hiatus in discourse, the being of the living subject, becomes a ground for abstraction, its state of nonbeing. Here discrete concrete labours are equivalenced via money and the market; their particular content or character is 'nothing' in this context, it doesn't count for anything. Hence 'X is nothing to Y' or 'X is anything to Y', it has no real connection. Here equivalencing occurs via a convenient placeholder or myth which reflects or mimics the doxa of the situation.

The somatic consequences of such a discursive hiatus or *vaciller* are alienation, anxiety and disorientation as the following discussion will show.

Examples of, in Merleau-Ponty's locution, such sense descending into nonsense would be the post-war crisis of social democracy of the late 70s which evidenced a culture of blame and later, the crisis of U.K. national identity vis á vis the E.U. In both cases, a project can no longer be made to mean in its existing form and scapegoating as the targeting of respectively, trade union action (the

---

[33] Both ontologies constitute a void in the discourse of the other but a void which is active in appropriating its other. As Sartre (1998, p.12) notes, nothingness or non-being 'haunts being'. Non-being has a range of related meanings in the present text, but the idea of real abstraction distances it from Sartre. Non-being in this discussion includes the ground of appropriation, the context in which abstraction takes place, the invisible repair work which enables formal discourse to function in concrete situations via placeholders and a lack/anxiety/ associated with the suppression of the subject from discourse.

'winter of discontent') and immigrants is manifest as the tangibility of social unease or anxiety. It may be that 'the EU' embodies a mythology[34], has become a placeholder for the failure of 'austerity politics' but space for a full analysis is beyond the scope of this discussion. The *vaciller* imbricated in these discursive events would suggest, following the previous discussion of the substitution of abstractions for lived realities, that signification does not take place purely on a level of signs but has somatic implications for its subjects.

The chapter therefore, *inter alia*, aims to demonstrate the damage caused by the repression of the subject in abstractional discourses and the related inadequacy of theories which assume that dominant discourses can be made to mean for individuals: that they win people over by sheer hegemonic/circulatory power. It is argued that individuals have a sense of self, a sedimented biographical structure of lived experience and that this operates as Gramsci (1971, p.324) notes: as 'an infinity of traces without an inventory', that tell us who we are.

The recuperation of selfhood normally works through discursive articulations of lived identities. However, in a situation where the ideological formation enters a crisis, articulation is voided and routes to identification become inaccessible. In such circumstances, it is argued, that ideologies function to displace lived experience in processes of self-identification.

A number of different illustrations will be examined to show that despite such a crisis of identity there a substantial sense of self against which ideological or discursive structures have to negotiate meaning. It will be suggested that general or particular institutional crises provoked by a loss of direction or disorientation in the face of new situations provide a good way of bringing out this experiential level of selfhood as suggested above it is under these circumstances that ideological or discursive formations of identity in institutional life melt away.

The contemporary anxieties about the body, the gender politics of the domestic sphere, colonialism and post-colonial identities provide illustrations of the general argument about anxiety and identity-disorientation produced by hegemonic fragmentation.

It will be in order first of all though to say something about the character of anxiety and its relation to the somatics of the social individual.

---

[34] Part of such a mythology would be 'Brussels bureaucrats'/'red tape', contributions to the EU budget as a kind of theft, invasion by foreigners and 'loss of sovereignty'.

The Production of Social Anxiety

Following Merleau-Ponty (1964, p.134) anxiety, *inter alia* would be experienced intersubjectively, the individual in its relation to others 'undergoes an objectivation' and

> is no longer just the epistemological subject pure being for itself...he (*sic*) is for others, and because of this he becomes generic subject.

Merleau-Ponty speaks of the way 'terror' is produced by the unravelling of the way individual projects are tied into the larger historical trends via their 'ambiguity and contingency'; projects never turn out the way we intend as their logic is never that of the individual but rather takes an intersubjective form. Consequently anxiety is not only experienced by the individual in situated personal terms but is manifest culturally, it works intersubjectively as the 'terrror' or 'malificence' of unravelling historical projects (Merleau-Ponty, 2001, p.94, Kruks, p.139). Here intersubjectivity is fractured and appears as otherness, a form of self-negation[35] although 'paradoxically' its form remains social.

It is argued that this unravelling is the context of pathological tendencies where groups are scapegoated or otherwise stigmatised and a generalised culture of blame develops in the attempt to displace insecurity/anxiety onto less powerful others. Gramsci has argued that in periods of historical vacuum and /or transition where there is a 'crisis of authority', and by implication, identity... the ruling class has lost its consensus, i.e., is no longer 'leading'

> ...the great masses have become detached from their traditional ideologies. The crisis consists precisely in the fact that the old is dying and the new cannot be born; in this interregnum a great variety of morbid symptoms appear (1971, pp.275–6).

---

[35] See, for example, Rustin's analysis of the hiatus around the intersection between personal and institutional practice in the challenging clinical situation discussed in Chapter 1.

It will be suggested here that we could generalise this point to kinds of situations, specific terrain, institutional sectors, where there is a loss of direction and where in some way the fabric of hegemonic culture is undermined.

Whilst ideological hegemony is basically 'political' it is intertwined with cultural factors that is, the way the state articulates with the wider social formation as the 'integral state' (ibid., pp.261-5). This is exemplified in policy re the family, sexuality, education or the notion of management as the generalised exercise of power in social institutions, the media as legitimising official frameworks for policy debate, and so on. Some of these are more formally organised from above but others such as hegemonic masculinity are implied in policy. The way these work at the molecular level is arguably more historically contingent, discursively ambiguous and relies on the existence of elective affinities of a 'spontaneous' sort which occur because of the historically sedimented traces of for example, masculinist practices in everyday communication, as will be argued below. Within this context, the interweaving of personal, institutional and state practices provides a sense or intentional history and when these start to unravel we get non-sense or 'terror', to use Merleau-Ponty's locution.

To put it simply, displacement processes are favoured by contexts of ideological vacuum, places which make no sense in themselves. Here the interweaving of personal and institutional history which otherwise establishes an element of the generic or reciprocal-interactional (social) individual actually generates non-being as lived experience. The angst inherent in this is captured in Sartre's (1982) conception of serial relationships, as organised by a mythical other, where the cohesion of a group depends on an always receding external point, rather than the intrinsic, mutually self-constituting activity of members.

Cohen: moral panics

Cohen (1973, pp.53–60) like Sartre, argues in effect that such folk devils represent a flight of meaning, objections made about their characterisation are likely to be met by a flight of meaning to another target. 'It's not only this but…' Similarly, Cooper and Laing's (1964 pp.123–4) account of Sartrean seriality suggests that any collectivity thus characterised is spurious in that it is a multiplicity in which each member is 'identical, interchangeable, inessential, separate and, and solitary'. Its unity is always elsewhere:

The Jew is not the type common to each particular example but the perpetual being beyond himself in the other. The members of a series are appendages, as it were, of their common fantasy object.

Likewise, Cohen (op. cit., pp. 53–4, 61–5) gives what are in effect endless lists of issues which the media, members of the public etc. related to the so-called youth problem. Hence wherever the series comes to rest its unity is insinuated, is thought to lie elsewhere.

By contrast, as Gramsci (loc. cit.) argues, in the case of incorporation in a hegemonic project individuals are interpellated through an appeal to their culturally sedimented biographies, that is, identities which are relatively mutually reinforcing, making cross references over a range of issues rather than constituted via the serial 'not only this' (receding other).

In sum, when social reality ceases to make sense for the participants in particular sectors, that is, articulation of lived experience within the hegemonic view has become problematic, moral panics, social anxiety and scapegoating fill the vacuum. The anxiety can be short-lived as in Cohen's study of the 'youth problem', or it can be an on-going, constituent of social reality as in the cases of sexism, racism or the value relation (see below).

Hence rule can be sustained via power generated not only through the recruitment of subjects to new projects but also through the mobilisation of the public to causes incapable of coherent articulation, through displacement to fantasy objects, those incapable of being described through relations to other identifiable entities because of their intrinsic referential indeterminacy ('it's not only this but…').[36]

Some Instances of the Collapse of Meaning and Generation of Anxiety

Sheila Rowbotham (1973, pp.4–6) gives an account of the invisibility of women, their lack of recognition in the dominant discourses of the 1950s–1970s (*plus ca change?*) which arguably amounts to a displacement of meaning. In other words, this was 'the problem that had no name' which affected those women whose material circumstances were reasonably comfortable, whilst for

---

[36] See also Fisher (2009, p.44ff) for a Žižekian account of infinite deferral as the 'Big Other'.

others it was compounded by poverty and its psychological effects. However, in both cases there was both a sense of vacuity, lack of meaningful projects and also a sense that selfhood depended on resisting dominant definitions of their roles. All this is suffused in an atmosphere of unease about identity which is expressed in a prediscursive way: a feeling of nothingness but also of 'unarticulated' resistances:

there is the switching off, the half-there swimmy feeling, the barriers around yourself and there is illness. (Rowbotham, op. cit., p.75).

The lack of discursive recognition is highlighted in the dominant belief that women's depression in a privatised urban environment can be cured by drugs as the contemporaneous advert suggests: 'She can't change her environment but you can change her mood with Serenid-D' (ibid., p.76), a statement which expresses so many of the issues of recognition; the failure to address women except as through men and vested interests of political economy of the urban environment!

However, the key point for this discussion is that this picture of the '50s through '70s and beyond captures a sectoral crisis of hegemony of masculine authority and its displacement as an 'urban problem'. This was a period which marked the demise of the family wage concept and challenged the post-war gender settlement. For instance, Wilson (1991, pp.17–18) argues, citing Mumford as an example, that male anxieties were at least partly about control of women's sexuality in the post-war city. Women's dissatisfaction and resistance was already a factor in the post-war western life…the hegemonic 'solution' is more tranquillisers! Here sense (grasp of the way things are going) develops dialogically in the more or less organised ways in which women contested the gender order and were increasingly able to reference it through feminist ideas.

Another fault-line in the hegemonic fabric is that of 'race'. Trade union leader Bill Morris, referring to William Hague's[37] speech about Britain becoming a 'foreign land' noted.

---

[37] Hague was Leader of the Opposition at the time and Morris chair of the Trades Union Congress.

It is indeed a foreign land where ordinary black British families wake up almost every morning to listen on the radio to descriptions of themselves they do not recognise (*The Guardian, 2001, p.4*).

Earlier identifications of the colonial/postcolonial and their somatic consequences were noted by Fanon (1971, p.200) in the '50s:

[Before the Algerian war of national liberation] the truth is that colonialism in its essence was already taking on the aspect of a fertile purveyor of psychiatric hospitals...

Because it is a systematic negation of the other person and a furious determination to deny the other person all attributes of humanity, colonialism forces the people it dominates to ask themselves the question constantly: "In reality, who am I?"

The personality is voided and the Algerian becomes mere natural background to the human presence of the French colonialists. In this way, the colonial occupation differs from other sorts of military domination/occupation (loc. cit.) The question of contestation is crucial to that of establishing who one is. Morever, when there is no contestation,

There is during this calm period of successful colonisation a regular and important mental pathology which is the direct product of oppression (ibid., p.201).

A National Schizophrenia Fellowship survey in the U.K. showed that Afro-Caribbean men are 12 times more likely to be diagnosed with schizophrenia than white men. (*The Big Issue*, 2001, p.34). As in the case of women's oppression the subject is naturalised and experiences a somatic void.

On another level of somatic insubstantiality, a piece of research on black civil servants showed they experienced themselves in modes of spectrality: they felt they were there (recognised existents) and yet not there! (Puwar, 2001, p.660ff). Mercer's (1994) work on black identities in the UK argues that black identity has depended importantly on establishing a black cultural space from which to be a recognised contestant of cultural hegemony.

Arguably, all these illustrate the point that one may have a sense of self beyond the reference of discourse/ideology and that its somatic presence is illustrated in the pathologies thrown up in the context of discourses of pseudo- or non-recognition. In either case, there is some kind of resistance to dominant discursive figurations of subjectivity.

Another instance of this can be found in the widespread current concern with the way consumer capitalism impinges on the management of the body. Here again, it has been argued that resistance to the cultural norms of global capital takes forms evidenced in pathological developments. Anorexia and bulimia are both ways of resisting body management, although this must be seen in its mediations via individual biography. Body management as a hegemonic formation in this phase of capitalism should again be seen via its displacements. Health, for example, is displaced by fitness which at the same time is equivalenced with body 'shape' and 'tone'. The recruitment and resistance to this form of body regime are illustrated in a visit to the gym:

Trainer: "You know what? We are going to get you thin."
"I don't want to be thin," I insisted. The aim was to get fit…I do not want to be thin. There is no 'real' me inside, struggling to squeeze out past all that flesh. This body, saddle bags, stomach rolls and all, is the 'real' me. If the trainer could cook me low-fat, high-fibre nutritious, meals every day, then possibly. Thin means changing my life. Do I have to? (Weir, 2001, p.70)

Hence fitness is assimilated to shape and proximity to masculinist discourses about women's bodies. Bordo, (1993, p.212) argues that there is '…anxiety about women's desires in periods when traditional forms of gender organisation are being challenged' and that masculinist discourses attempt to gain control over women's bodies as a consequence of this.

Susan Bordo's (1993) account of periods of disruption in patriarchal culture and the anxiety this generates could usefully be read in terms of existential anxiety with the added insights that anxiety is not something subjective focussed on an external anxiety promoting object but is rather part of a shared (intersubjective) reality, where the subject's (generic) being for others becomes abstractional, colonised and external and hence threatening non-being to the experiential individual subject. The importance of this insight is that it locates non-being and anxiety, as the lived experience, texture, of the historical process.

In line with this, Bordo (1993, pp.185–6) argues that discursive control should not be seen as focussing on the 'other', the marginalisation of the powerless, as this 'obscures' the ordinary character of the process of normalisation and naturalisation[38]. The experience of the othered as part of a normalising strategy is also therefore 'generic' that is, shared by the non-othered. A focus on the othered implies the marginality of discursive power rather than its pervasiveness. The 'normality' of the experiences of the body, 'race' and gender discussed in this chapter should be borne in mind. Hence relations between dominant and subordinate groups in the context of contestation and conjunctural or sectoral hegemonic crisis are characterised by attempts to displace 'generic' anxiety onto subordinates; subordinates have problems, inadequacies and so on. (In Bordo's terms, this would be to 'de-normalise' them). The attempts at 'displacement' of these intersubjective experiences of historical disjuncture will, as before, be a major concern of the cases discussed here. Further, for Bordo, anxieties about the body have a generic quality in that 'the physical body...may symbolically reproduce central vulnerabilities and anxieties of the social body' (ibid., p.186).

The gym illustration given by Weir indicates how Bordo's basically Foucauldian account might be supplemented: resistance to dominant definitions of health and body management might reside in the somatics of biographical experience, in that to feel at home with the identity on offer, the woman in question observes that she'd have to 'change her life, that is, have a different kind of biographical trajectory.

The construction and contestation of subjectivity in modern capitalism

The discussion now turns to examine the structuring processes through which meaning is negotiated in modern capitalism. There is a tendency, often associated with social constructionism as suggested in du Gay's (2008, pp.48–9) reading of Weber's personhoods, roles and so on, to view discursive practice in modernity as somehow complete in itself rather than drawing on, negotiating lived experience. It is as if the institutional agencements navigated by human beings have uni-directional transformative power over the latter. In this case, new forms of discursive practice are always already generalised, as if magicked into existence as *faits accompli*. Discourses signifying a translation to new conjunctural arrangements are seen as introducing new ways of identifying things which occlude past or more localised meanings. This view ignores the

---

[38] In Bordo's case this 'obscures the normalising function of technologies of diet and body management' (loc. cit.).

impact, as argued in Chapter 2, of the synthesis required to translate past hegemonic constructions to new fields of reference, social worlds, and tends to see the problem of mystification or discursive power in almost manichaen terms of total administration and its à la carte discourses where institutional language and practice annihilates past experience as an epistemological rupture and temporal disjuncture.

In contradistinction to this, it is argued here that some emphasis should be placed on past modes of practice and the way that these are employed, drawn upon, in attempts to articulate the unfolding present. As reified history, past experiences in effect remain ruins, as Benjamin has argued, emburdened with a content they cannot disclose as the context of reference, conjunctural alignment and so on, shifts. A grasp of this development requires a new representational space, but this is a contested space as modern capitalism attempts to recuperate its hegemony.

Jameson (1991, p.19) has identified ways in which recuperation of the past in modern capitalism might occur and how this leads to the expression of somatic anxiety. He has for instance noted a lack or longing which issues in a form of desire ideologically expressed in what he terms the 'nostalgia mode'. Here, for example, abstractions ('imaginary and stereotypical idealities') figure as past aesthetic styles, detached from their historical context, conveying pastness which become emburdened with affective attachments: pure form rather than form synthesised with content. This is also emblematic of commodity culture as a closed, self-referential world of abstraction as *inter alia* in the example of body management and its disjunction with lived experience. We now turn to examine Benjamin for a possible way out of the circle of abstraction.

Benjamin: Fragmentation, Phantasmagoria and Recuperation

Buck-Morss, (1989, pp. 159–61) notes that Benjamin has argued that the over-conventionalisation and petrification of images hollows them out and as ruins of their former presences, their fragments coalesce to reveal an excess of meaning that was in former times in effect sutured[39] from the knowing subject. Benjamin sees fragmentation as framed by *Gestalt*[40] which in effect exposes the

---

[39] 'Suture' is used here in the non-Lacanian sense developed in Chapter 1.

[40] Khatib (op. cit., pp. 1–2) suggests that Gestalt (like synthesis in Chapter 2) faced with

fragment to suppressed determinants/mediations of its context of production. The space created by the tensions of fragmentation and which are experienced in *Gestalt* suggest a form of Husserlian quasi-perception through which the abstract/fragmentary assimilation of modernity can be subverted. Quasi-perceptions can be thought of as 'threshold experiences', intimations or grounds of perception (Khatib, op.cit., pp.6–7). For example, a sense of disorientation, mimicry, the uncanny, mirage, ambiguity through which a gap in signification can be revealed, an 'image space' where a contesting form of representation might be formulated. Such perceptional features eventuate from an oscillation between the sensuous and the abstractional, 'occult' effect of capital as a 'purely social relation' on the sensuous, to produce the 'real surreal' (ibid., p.6), reminiscent of the idea of abstractional *vaciller* discussed in Chapter 2. What is novel here though is the thought that the materials of abstraction might themselves form the basis of non-reified perception; the supposition that the fragments themselves may offer a route through and beyond the occult nature of abstraction, that the new may issue from a *Gestalt* experience within the material of reification itself. [41]

For Benjamin, it is the everyday which grounds the occult nature of abstraction just as the abstraction proves impervious, opaque to the everyday, appears in a continuum of the everyday as the familiar, more of the same.

Any serious exploration of occult, phantasmagoric gifts and phenomena presupposes a dialectical entwinement, we penetrate the mystery only to the degree we recognise it in the everyday world, by virtue of a dialectical optic

---

commodification undergoes dissolution or 'de-formation' rather than, as argued earlier, translation of a content to new social worlds, projects etc. and that it is in the dissolving of the Gestalt that threshold experiences occur, a fleeting sense of double-take, and so on. Gestalt/translation as a process is interrupted and dissolved. Gestalt,. as Riceour (1986, pp.299), Waldron, (op.cit., p.167) have argued for metaphor, has a resembling trope suggesting mimic forms of an as yet inchoate object, reference whose formation is blocked in this case.

[41] Whilst musical genres such as Punk or Reggae which via commodification have come to function as autonomous categories whose effect is to occlude the reception of their actual content – Benjamin's insight means that within a Gestalt or open horizon their affinities might be realised in a synthesis such as 'white reggae' (The Clash, and so on).

that perceives the everyday as impenetrable, the impenetrable as everyday (Benjamin GS 11, cited in Khatib, op. cit., p.6).

It is this very *Gestalt* quality of the everyday which suggests a way out, the assimilation of abstraction to the already known and judged accordingly. The Surreal here appears in the horizon of its real, lived production and consequent perceptual juddering, a critique which invokes its spectral or mimic status.

Intimations of the new

As argued above, over-conventionalised, petrified symbols offer only a trace, a pointer, and it is the awareness of this that facilitates a hermeneutics of the context or constellation which enlivened them (Buck-Morss, op. cit., pp.159–61). The fragments therefore only function allegorically, thus imbuing images with the power of invisible meanings. As such, here meaning becomes arbitrary and substitutable/equivalenced arbitrarily, in a way reminiscent of stereotyping, creating, as Adorno notes, images of 'wish and anxiety' (ibid., pp.181–2). As the 19th Century progresses, Benjamin suggest this sensibility intensifies. The production of objects/commodities accelerates and with it the voids or arbitrariness of signification. Hence commodification entails that

With the vitiation of their use value, the alienated things are hollowed out and, as ciphers they draw in meanings. It should be kept in mind that, in the nineteenth century, the number of hollowed out things increases at a rate and on a scale that was previously unknown, for technical progress is continually withdrawing newly introduced objects from circulation (Benjamin, 1999, p.466).

A concomitant of this increasing ubiquity of material things is an accentuation of the spectral sensibility, moreover, the oversubstantial world of fragmented relations and things (a positivistic ethos), and spectrality are two sides of the same coin. A collectively negotiated way through the reified world is however offered via the 'ghosts of material things' (Nerval) and 'the spaces of lost times embedded in the spaces of material things' (ibid., xii).

This double-sidedness of the fragment shows that whilst the effects of fragments or sediments of past practices on the present in the fetishistic appropriation of experience can be seen as the rule of abstraction it is also important to recognise that over-burdening of the symbolism of past discourses with a content they are inadequate to express, a discursive hiatus, represents a generic experience of self-estrangement which may also be an opening onto the image spaces of critique and political contestation. Buck-Morss (op. cit., pp.284–6) similarly argues that the fantasies of Benjamin's 'dreamworld' are shared imaginings, not sutured from the collectivity. The fragmentedness of 'official' identities may form the basis of new, hybrid articulations of subjectivity. [42]

For example, Hall (1997, p.58) notes, that the experience of the Afro-Caribbean diaspora is increasingly used to re-articulate the codes of the dominant culture. It is a narrative of displacement that relies on 'a certain imaginary plenitude', a sense of place and belonging which is only expressed indirectly through the processes of cultural syncretisation which produce black English, black British cinema etc. Here the fantasy becomes concretised in a shared culture, a synthesis or *Gestalt* through which 'English' is translated as culture into new social worlds where the abstractions of colonial classification are repositioned and hybridised, mutually transformed. This is encapsulated by Mercer:

> Across a whole range of cultural forms, there is a 'syncretic' dynamic which critically appropriates elements from the master-codes of the dominant culture and 'creolises' them. The subversive force of this hybridising tendency is most apparent at the level of language itself where creoles, patois and black English decentre, destabilise and carnivalise the linguistic domination of 'English'. (Mercer, 1988, cited ibid., p.58).

Benjamin's comments (Leslie, 2000, pp. 119–22) on the emergence of the new as phantasmagoria, suggest how these shared imaginings might function in relation to existing symbolic resources. Hence, it can be claimed that the other side of linguistic decrepitude and fractured senses is the emergence of senses appropriate to our present practices as projects, intentional objects, as in the case of Black Englishness. The ability to move beyond collective imaginings to the

---

[42] Recent discussion of the trends towards 'glocalisation' sometimes focus on diversity of outcomes rather than process and thereby overlook the synthesis required to produce diversity, new or different things are not just discrete entities but represent a living fusion of existing cultural trends. See Feather (2016, p.330) on cross fertilisation of music genres.

expression of new social forms becomes, as Mercer (1994) has argued, a question of cultural politics.

The problem of subjects' inability to name their experiences, to access their discursive representation, is then the problem of hegemonic contestation between these incipient meanings and the ones passing into 'meaninglessness', nostalgic desuetude. That is, a struggle ensues between subjects' ability to express their experiences in new, liberating ways and the 'pathological' attempts of the *ancien regime* to hold the semantic line. For example, the U.K.'s Brexit debate has unleashed new fantasy objects of anxiety and xenophobia around the myths of nation state and national identity as placeholders in a re-elaboration of the hegemonic order.[43]

'Meaningless' terms can be revived by a process of displacement, as suggested above, the accretion of new meanings which are compacted with older ones such that, to take another theme examined here, the older question of women's autonomy as a threat to social order, posed by Mumford and others can reappear in the guise of bodily control along the lines of Bordo's (1993) argument about body culture being a displacement of women's control over their bodies. Hegemonic masculinity gains new life via bodily commodification. The aim of autonomy in effect dynamises 'body culture' through the practices of body shaping, building and control although its intentionality is at the same time fractured and disfigured by its abstractional appropriation.

From phantasmagoria to formal rationality via the unconscious

As Rustin indicates in Chapter 1, the hiatus in institutional discursive practice represented by borderline states is an intersection between institutional structure as bureaucratic fragmentation and the unconscious. It shows the anchorage of institutional life in the part – objects of the latter. In that sense, it shows the embodiment of classification systems and formal rationality in the object world of the unconscious and as mutually constitutive of the discursive crises. In other words, it shows fantasy and discursivity as interactive parts of the production of social anxiety.

The doxic basis of hollowed-out images allows the equivalencing of the latter in a way that draws on the doxa to reinforce stereotyping and myth which lies

---

[43] See, for instance, "UK has seen Brexit-related growth in racism," says UN representative.
https://www.theguardian.com/politics/2018/may/11

outside bureaucracy but which the latter unconsciously draws on in framing or negotiating critical gaps in its discourse, as is argued here and previous chapters. Hence the difficulty in throwing off stereotypical thinking lies in that it is not just 'subjective' prejudice but also anchored in the institutional life of, for instance, the nation state. As argued above, it exists in the fantasy (part) objects of the unconscious, which, as Benjamin (Khatib, op. cit., p. 2) notes, are not distinct as phantasms from the real (fetish) world of abstraction but overlap with it; the phantasy world is real insofar as it mutually constitutes the fetish/occult world of modern capitalism. In the U.K., we can see the phantasms of the part-object played out in, for instance, the limited immigration status of Commonwealth Citizens, the oversight of the Windrush generation, the 'Hostile environment' policy. They all operate via an intersection between institutional state discourse and unconscious fantasy where the integrity of the latter is threatened. The elision of the unconscious object world with its bureaucratic interpellation in formal citizenship eventuates in the association of racial subalternity with groups that threaten this borderline or placeholder in the narrative of 'nation-state'.

Importantly, we can see from the above that by operating fetishistically, signification can provide new life for decrepit practices via abstractional recruitment of their hidden, displaced meaning structures. A useful parallel here can perhaps be found in Marx's metaphorical encapsulation: capitalism operates via an alienation, the displacing of living labour whilst at the same time depending on its use value; it is living labour that animates dead capital.[44]

Spectrality, Living Labour and the Commodity Form

The process of displacement represented by hegemonic crisis and reworking owes something, we have argued, to the appearance of aspects of reality as sutured fragments which insinuate rather than reference a series of meanings as 'literal' in the sense of being immediate, obvious, common sense and so on. A spectral charge is produced by this process, it is argued, because in abstractional displacement a colonisation of the everyday or doxic takes place through which

---

[44] We get a sense of this romance with the vampiric from Marx, Capital, Vol.1, p.80, where he notes 'The whole mystery of commodities, all the magic and necromancy that surrounds the products of labour as long as they take the form of commodities, vanishes as soon as we come to other forms of production.'

the doxa or trace is mimicked. This 'representation' or *vaciller* gives the particularity of the doxa the appearence of universality and hence of immediacy as valid both 'here' and 'everywhere' at the same time. Consequently, in abstractional discourse this obviousness appears as a spectral investment, the absence/hiatus of contextual determinations/allusions which would give the latter coherent expression, that is, in a way that would identify its topic.

In the above section, the usefulness of Benjamin's phantasmagoria to unpicking abstractional displacement has been explored. The discussion now turns to aspects of the phantasmagoria in Arthur's examination of the 'spectre of value', in particular the ideas of masks, personifications, supports and the unarticulated, invisible subjectivity behind these which exists in forms of self-estrangement.

We can find a parallel process to the cultural displacements[45] we have discussed in Arthur's (2001) treatment of the value form where money takes on the role of the serial entity whose meaning is always a concretion beyond itself in the infinitely exchangeable particularities that it represents. As with the fragment which displaces the lived reality, occults the world of concrete things and relations, money takes precedence over lived particularities:

And what is money but the empty universal that not only 'stands for' real wealth but elbows it aside and takes precedence? (ibid., p.41)

Further, the spectral presence, capital, is only 'halo, mirage, a semblance of actuality' (loc. cit.). Commodification communicates this effect to whatever it touches.

---

[45] Arthur, (op. cit., p.42, f.12) notes that Marx describes the relation between concrete and abstract labour as one of Verrückung. This, Arthur suggests enables Marx to draw on the double meaning of its conceptualisation, that is as displacement and madness (derangement). Importantly for our argument about the generality of the logic of commodification this also captures the sense of cultural displacement in the preceding discussion. This sense is also rendered by Fowkes in his translation of Vol. 1 where Verrückung appears as 'this absurd form' of labour (Arthur, loc. cit., Fowkes, 1991, p.169). Just as the worker is unable to recognise themselves in the products of their labour, in the 'cultural' argument, we are confronted by our own intentionality in a guise where it ceases to make sense but at the same time it continues to animate our senseless orientation.

The spectre inhabits such material as a secret subject, animating it, and, vampire-like, communicating spectrality to all with which it has intercourse. Under the hegemony of the spirit world of capital, the phenomenal subject is itself a spectre. We exist for each other only as its instances, its 'personifications', 'masks', 'supports', to use Marx's terms (loc. cit.).

Du Gay's (2008, pp.45–50) comments on the arrival of abstraction in the form of legal-rational bureaucracy echo Marx's delineation of capitalism, in that for du Gay abstraction manifests itself through the adoption of formal roles, 'personhoods' with a contractual status which are independent of the concrete individual and tie in with Elias's notion of the *homo clausus* or discrete individual (outside the social nexus). Abstraction breaks up the socially bonded (interrelational) world by positing an independent reality of exchangeable roles and values.

Similarly, in our case of the fetishised conventional term, the decrepit signifier feeds off the living content which it displaces. Hence in the example of the body as a mechanism of social control masculinist meanings displace other meanings of the body. The masculinist discourse is the invisible charge around the signifiers of health, fitness, 'shape' etc. and through them regenerates its hegemonic power and thus renders health, fitness etc. as something other than what we understand them to be, but without saying so.

The process of displacement engenders meaninglessness in that things are invested with meanings which because of their spectrality we cannot grasp: the structures of reception of this phenomenal subject fail to transmit the sutured content. Hence things 'mean other than they should' and so our anxiety at this dislocation of sense. Marx's account of fetishism in *Capital* (Marx, 1974, p.77) picks out these features of spectrality in the misrecognition of production as the capital relation. 'In that world, the productions of the human brain appear as independent beings endowed with life, and entering into relation with one another and the human race', and again:

the relation of the producers to the sum total of their own labour is presented to them as a social relation, existing not between themselves, but between the products of their labour and this is an objective character stamped upon the product of that labour (loc. cit.).

Hence the production process assumes an objective character over and against the producers, whatever one's sense of that process is as the production of use values.

Spectrality does not therefore imply that people simply fail to grasp the reference/identity of things, but rather that their sense of them is fractured. This is not merely a point about structuralist or phenomenological decentering of meaning as in spectrality meaning fragments have no definite structure/logic in lived reality but rather that they function as one thing masquerading as another and animated by it. The social appears as the individual and vice versa, rather than there being a social individual, for instance.

Again, it is not simply a displacement of one meaning by another: this occurs in everyday dialogical situations where the pattern is 'this, not that is the problem'. Whilst this embodies investment in identities and power, dialogically, there is no necessary relation between these and the spectrality of the commodity form.

Marx identifies the production of capital as involving the occurrence of events in two separate worlds (Arthur, op. cit., p.40), one which recognises commodities as its reference point and another which takes use value as its anchorage in reality. The processes that operate within the world of commodities are located by Marx as having their own logic. Hence both sides of this commodity-actuality divide operate according to ascertainable rules. It is only when the divide is straddled as it necessarily is in the production of value and its concomitant contractual exchange relations, the twin mutually constitutive faces of capitalist modernity, that spectrality or incoherence arises. Whilst Arthur's work on spectrality emphasises the haunting of the lived relations, he makes a more general point that extraction of value has its non-being in the 'real…process of transformation of use values' (loc. cit.). Elsewhere Lefebvre (2006, pp.24–5) notes a double haunting where the quotidian and modern 'mark and mask each other'.[46]

In the world of lived relations, the somatic consequence of non-being is incoherence or discursive hiatus, the alienation or fetishistic experience of work and life in general. If the model is applied in the 'more cultural' way, we can see

---

[46] As Cunningham (2005, pp. 18–19) notes however, the idea of abstraction as a real world of relations is not developed by Lefebvre. Another variant of haunting, as possession, in this case, is found in Habermas's (1999, p.173) idea of a reverse colonisation of system by lifeworld.

the incoherencies as lying in the attempt to map ideas which had some real purchase but have now been hollowed out by abstraction onto changed realities. Here they function as abstractional placeholders to equivalence aspects of the experiential, as the previous examples suggest.

This mapping of fantasy objects onto the world often compounds the initial sense of crisis, as in moral panics where reaction to a 'problem' serves to produce its amplification (cf. Cohen, op. cit., pp. 203–4). There is at this point a temporal hiatus between our developing projects and those of hegemonic desuetude. Things make no sense in that they convey involuntary invisible meanings but then sense is 'retrieved' spectrally as the oversubstantial world of sutured hidden investments.

'Race' and Hegemonic Contestation in the Senior Civil Service

The final illustration of spectrality examines the incoherence threatened by the presence of the black senior civil servant and the production of anxiety where white universality as a taken for granted of civil service modus vivendi passes into desuetude and its meaning structures break up. As a contesting presence, Puwar (2001, pp. 659-60) notes that black senior civil servants effect disorientation of the established white culture, they are 'space invaders' who 'disturb the white serenity of the body politic' (p.657) thus challenging the white spatial somatic norm. Following Puwar (op. cit., pp. 655–6), this threat to the white norm is countered by a displacement of black identity such that black subject positions are imbued with the decrepit subalternity or 'infantilism' of colonial discourse. The 'universality' of whiteness (Puwar, op. cit., p.656 ff), really a fragment (or, in Freudian parlance, a part-object), lingers on. Thus the problematisation of whiteness in postcoloniality is displaced as black subalternity. White anxiety about (white) universality in a context of multiculturalism is translated into an inability to see actual black civil servants as peers.

The effect of whiteness, the white civil service etc., as a fetishistic object is the naturalisation and normalisation of the meanings this stereotypical image insinuates but cannot disclose (Hall, 1997, p.258) as it consolidates white hegemony. The middle class, male linguistic codes and mannerisms of 'white Englishness' are the sedimented, unspoken content which informs the obvious, literal, neutral, 'universal' atttributes of the Senior Civil Service. As Hall (op.

cit., p.268) argues fetishised forms of symbolism work not by speaking their name but by insinuating, haunting the 'cover-story' or more literal understanding, the conventional designation, and in this case the placeholder 'bureaucratic neutrality'. The solidity or naturalness of the fetishistic object lies, as indicated above, in its suturing from the background context or subscript. In this way, the subliminal 'white' quality of the civil service acts to naturalise a very particular sense of universality and hegemony.

Discourse, disorientation and the possible recuperation of identity

Following the argument that hegemonic crisis, in this case that of post-coloniality, fractures identity, the price of fetishised displacement, into the fantasy object of a 'neutral', unraced civil service by this discursive form of power is lack of identity and anxiety for both whites and minorities. Discursive power enables this to be transferred from one group to the other as a process of (fantastic) normalisation (see Cohen's op. cit., pp.203–4, description of the processes of marginalisation and consolidation of norms, social control etc.). Agents have an investment in the identities conveyed in the process of hegemonic contestation as it relates to sense of biographical trajectory. In other words, the 'traces or sediments without an inventory' Gramsci observes provide an excess of meaning over any stated identity. This has ramifications beyond the phenomenal subject enunciated by the value form to the domain of lived-through experience because, as is argued above, anxiety is a condition of the *somatics* of the self taken as an intersubjective, generic construct. [47]

Black identities are undercut in these circumstances of contestation and may be constrained to mimic their white peers and in that sense represent a difference and a threat (Bhabha cited in Puwar, 2001, p.667). However, the threat which is germane to this discussion stems not so much from the mimicry itself and consequent disavowal or displacement of experiential selfhood required for success in the civil service but from what is insinuated within mimicry by black spectrality due to the agency of an unstated excess of meaning re post-coloniality and multiculturalism which the black senior civil servant carries with them. In

---

[47] 'The generic' here does not equate to a homogeneous form of subjectivity. Rather, the intersubjective denotes a dialogical, hybrid entity. A shift or translation from the positioning within one social world to that of another, as argued in Chapter 2, involves a synthesis as part of a translation or metaphoric transfer between the two discursive positions.

other words, this is the occulted moment of a contesting, appropriating presence rather than purely that of a subaltern positioning. To use the Bakhtinian (Hall, op. cit. pp.293–4) insight, it is the moment in which Englishness is stolen from the mouths of those who traditionally enunciate it and takes on a different, 'dialogical' meaning which is perhaps suggested by the inclusion of Linton Kwesi Johnson in the Penguin Book of English Verse. In this case, however, unlike the fantasised 'white' civil service it is genuinely possible to articulate the sedimented suggestiveness, this unstated excess of meaning with a living discourse of post-coloniality as a present reality. Hence the relationship between black and white forms of spectrality here is asymmetrical. Whilst both may be features of the rationalisation of the modern world, one is tied to the hollowing out inherent to racialised forms of hegemony whilst the other, so to speak, represents the genetic presence of the Black Atlantic in the construction of the West.

Interrelations between white and minority groups translate the 'colonial' abstractions such that on the one hand the dominant group displaces, renders invisible, black spectrality as white 'universality' but experiences a counter to this in that white identity is also mediated by its displaced 'other'. In other words, *inter alia*, white identity is experienced through the 'lack' represented by black presence, through the subjectivity and desire of the other. The effect of black spectrality is therefore to contest the subsumption of 'the other' and in Benjamian terms, to create an image space or quasi-perception. Puwar's (2001, p.658) work is suggestive in this respect – the experience of abstractional positioning as 'not there' (invisibility), dissonance, disorientation, subalternisation, hyper-observation, and so on, is arguably also a window through which new forms of subjectivity can be created. As suggested in Chapter 2 such translations require an initial synthesis with the other's field of reference. The intersubjective character of hegemonic hiatus and its anxieties can be thus traced as a blocking of this, a point of *vaciller*. At the interactional level, the generic anxiety is, needless to say, displaced by the hegemonic group, projected as the fantasy part-objects of their inner world onto the black senior civil servants who consequently experience themselves in modes of spectrality, invisibility, mimicry of, in effect, 'not being there'.[48] (See Puwar, 2001, the section 'The Burden of Invisibility').

---

[48] In Benjamin's perspective, the fantasy objects of the unconscious are just as real as the fragmented 'external' world of social relations. (Khatib, op. cit., p. 2)

As suggested above, the generation of the image space can be further elaborated in terms of the oscillations (*vaciller*) through which the 'other' appears as surreal, as concrete universality, naturalised, eternal. At the same time, black bodies appear as invisible, as assimilated via mimicry to the white somatic norm. In other words, as Puwar (2004, p. 143, citing Goldberg, 1997) notes, abstractions ('stereotypes') operate where the lived experience of the black senior civil servant is at once hidden and at the same time experienced as an abstraction, a form of visibility as self-estrangement:

> The effect of the simultaneous enactment of visibility and invisibility of black bodies is such that race hides those it is projected to mark and illuminates those it leaves unmarked.

It is thus part of a complex process of 'othering' which rests on a hiatus in civil service culture, the invisibility or absence of the white norm in its formal discourse. Othering

> occurs in relation to the 'centrifugal somatic norm'. This social process enables whites, and especially white men, those who are unmarked and yet illuminated as 'the norm of humanity' to masquerade as the 'ghosts of modernity'

The lived and the abstractional thus function as two moments of modernity, the abstraction hides in the lived bodies of its subjects, whilst these in turn provide the living subscript through which the (white) 'neutral' civil service is situated and functions, as Puwar's (2001, p.664) account indicates[49]. The black presence in 'these white elite positions is dependent on their acceptance of the invitation to masquerade and 'mimic' whiteness' however, these self-inscriptions remain 'ambiguous and unassimilable' (to the white somatic norm/lifeworld).

Whilst Puwar (loc. cit.) notes in the case of Fanon's account of mimicry that his performance in white spaces 'masked over' his 'Creoleness', or hybridity, Fanon's (1973, p. 77) narrative also indicates the possibility of recuperation.

---

[49] 'The (white) abstract civil servant', and so on (ibid., p.657).

The movements, attitudes, the glances of the others fixed me there in the sense that a chemical solution is fixed by a dye. I was indignant; I demanded an explanation. Nothing happened. I burst apart. Now the fragments have been put together again by another self.

Again,

...Not yet white, no longer black, I was damned...What was broken to pieces was rebuilt, reconstructed by the intuitive lianas of my hands (ibid., pp.97–8).

Hence although the colonial gaze shattered its subjects, here Fanon's fragments of selfhood, in all their Western otherness, are reassembled in new syncretic identities. A similar point was argued by Mercer[50] in relation to Black Englishness where it's suggested that hybridity is a subversive contesting moment of abstractional dominant 'articulations', a particular example of a more general argument about hybridity as a suppressed aspect of selfhood in identitarian hegemonic formations. This insight has of course somatic implications in the current argument as it highlights the contrast between a multicultural sense of renewal of selfhood and the anxieties/nostalgia denoted by the empty, abstractional signifiers of Brexit's 'Olde England' etc.

Arguably then, recognising the fracturing of experience represented in the fetishistic image or fantasy object provides a framework for understanding the deprivation of meaning, mutual acknowledgement and sense of place/ontological security which are heightened features in global capitalism.

However, it also provides a way of seeing the fragility of fetishised structures of experience and how they might be contested via the contradictory nature of such experience as at once everyday open biographical horizon and commodification in which the fragments of the latter are reconfigured (as Fanon suggests) in the trajectory of the former.

---

[50] Elsewhere Mercer (1995, p.28) stresses Fanon's view that the colonial body 'is fragmented, dismembered. 'an object in the midst of other objects' a view perhaps consonant with Benjamin's idea of the generation of the image space, given Fanon's suggestion of a recuperation of selfhood from colonial reification.

Concluding Reflections

Whilst most discussion of exclusion and marginalisation in modern capitalist societies has focused on the relations between dominant and subordinate groups the chapter has sought to look behind this to the institutional complexes which frame such power and economic differentials. To do this it has been necessary to draw out the nature of the modern capitalist state and the way it equivalences individuals and their projects abstractly, that is, without regard to the particularity of the cases/values involved. The contract the individual forms with the state is by definition based on abstractional subsumption of the individual and therefore unequal exchange relations and these validate market relations, that is, the latter are mediated by the juridical notion of contract which guarantees and equivalences the (unequal) values exchanged.

In sum, the unequal exchange relations as argued from both phenomenology and Marxism, are abstractional relations which are derivative of lived relations and subsumption is not therefore purely about differentials of income, wealth, status and power but about the production of a world which lives a ghostly derivative existence within the world it subsumes. It is, arguably, within this framework that capital and the state develop the abstractional hierarchies and specialisms of a division of labour.

To continue, exchange relations, as Weber (du Gay, 2008) suggested, are based on identifying not individuals as such but roles or personhoods they might adopt in order to subsist within the social worlds they are part of. Marx (see above) amplifies the argument about the effects of exchange relations when he observes that exchange relations within capitalism appear as a social relation but one which excludes the individual! The market ensures that this is not 'the relation of the producers to the sum total of their labour' but rather one exclusively 'between the products of their labour'. It is only as mediated by this market abstraction that the individual worker appears and then as a personhood, which is state-guaranteed, defined contractually, an intertwining of the abstractions of state and market.

Thus the elaboration or unpacking of abstractions from contract and market allows us to arrive at the 'individual'. The relation between this individual as *homo clausus* and its validation by social groups is then raised. The work of Gramsci enables us to see how this relation can be legitimated. The notion of the integral state which encompasses not just the formal structures of the state but the 'voluntary' peer-based relations of civil society co-opts the latter such that the everyday institutional life seems to require the very qualities of peer relations to function, a kind of bogus spontaneity or 'team spirit' within contractual life. Modern capitalist society thus validates itself by an anchorage in civic life and thus mediates and substitutes itself for civic life and concrete class etc. relations. The other side of this is that there is always a subscript to the arbitrary (neutral) institutional complex of the modern state such that its arbitrariness apropos concrete life is a situated arbitrariness, and the neutrality a masquerade. The state subsists on the basis of what it subsumes in the guise of neutrality. The capitalist hegemonic bloc 'haunts' the state but at the same time is rendered abstractional by it, producing the kinds of personhoods required for exchange relations, as mentioned above. The state in modern capitalism thus mediates other forms of subsumption, including those of women, minorities, class, the individual and so on by the production of requisite abstractions. The subjectivity of the black senior civil servant, for example, is displaced or subsumed by a personhood abstracted from the interactional world of white middle class Oxbridge[51] life.

In terms of the wider context of hegemonic crisis and marginalisation, the state plays a key role in the marginalisation and stigmatisation of minority groups as seen in the U.K.'s ambivalence towards the rights of the Windrush children generation or again, those of E.U. citizens in the context of the Brexit scenario, a form of de-individualisation or delegitimation which has led to their zmeaninglessness, a lack in search of the perpetually deferred other.

---

[51] See Puwar (2001, p. 666) on the 'very Oxbridge type' ethos of the senior civil service.

4

Language, Power and Ideology

Generally...our society takes the greatest pains to conjure away coding of the narrative situation [that is, the living context of narrativisation-H.F.]: there is no counting the number of narrational devices which seek to naturalise the subsequent narrative by feigning to make it the outcome of some natural circumstance and thus, as it were, 'disinaugurating it'. The reluctance to declare its codes characterises bourgeois society and the mass culture issuing from it: both demand signs which do not look like signs. Narration has an ambiguous role; it gives onto the world in which the narrative is undone (consumed), whilst at the same time it closes the narrative, constitutes it definitively. (Barthes, 1977, p.117).

This discussion will examine the idea that closed ('literal') or readerly (Barthes, 2004, p.4) forms of discourse operate to displace agents' shared meanings, living language.

The chapter suggests parallels between the commodification or abstraction of everyday life and the rendering of language into what Barthes identifies as a readerly mode of communication and in this way it extends the idea of 'he readerly', that is, sees it as an aspect of abstraction. In formal institutional settings of modern capitalism, both of these are argued to involve processes of displacement and colonisation, to use Habermas's (1999) term.

The discussion is framed by the claim made by Dummett, (see below) that living or 'natural' language always requires a moment of conventionalisation or classification in order to facilitate identification of its topic.

Hence ultimately the discussion hinges on the role of codification, the conventional in speech; whether it necessarily results in the displacement of living language into readerly discourse or alternatively that it can mediate everyday language without semantic closure. It is argued that displacement as an effect of modern capitalism is a special case, a spectral inhabitation where the grounds of communication, its context, disappear in a process of 'naturalisation' of speech. The ability of structures of modernity to effect such displacement is a manifestation of the institutional power to circulate meanings via discursive formations and their 'net-like organisation' (Foucault, 1986, p.234).

This can be better understood by recourse to the performative nature of institutional structure and language within such formal contexts where social practice involves fragmenting specialisms, hierarchisation and consequent bureaucratic secrecy. Bureaucratic compartmentalisation and its discrete knowledges, thus leads to antinomies or dualisms in the production of discourse and knowledge.[52]

Dead Texts and Living Language: Abstraction and Its Metaphorical Counter – A Framework for the Discussion

Readerly or literal forms of signification are clearly related to processes of repetition, which themselves indicate an ability or power to produce and circulate meanings. Such textbook, codified language which demonstrates how to interpret signs (texts, symbols) remains abstract in relation to contextual identifications. We're all supposed to grasp what 'pay here' etc. means regardless of cultural variation. Despite its abstractness, it is, arguably, none the less real in that discursive practices function at this level of (literal) meaning. In economic exchange, customers are involved in processes of exchange proceeding in a way which expresses the abstract equivalence, exchange value between commodities, and so on. Hence in both linguistic and economic cases there is a kind of false or misplaced concreteness (Halewood, 2013, pp.159) involved in the exchange. Both appear to invoke a directness or immediacy which in fact relies on the suppression of a mediating context of exchange or communication; money or text function as mediations but here appear as autonomous embodiments of value or meaning.

The 'literal', as a linguistic phenomenon, it will be argued, turns out to be something of a chimera[53] which while posing as concrete, immediate communication in fact, following an homology with Arthur's (2001)

---

[52] See Feather (2016, p.332) on antinomialism in institutional social science.

[53] See de Certeau (1988) cited below on the 'faceless' quality of the literal.

characterisation of the relation between abstract and living labour, displaces concrete or living language but maintains a spectral presence within it. Hence, to further reproduce Arthur's (loc. cit.) framework, 'the literal' does not exist[54] as a concrete feature of any utterance but its non-being haunts living language through its mobilisation of everyday typifications, the cultural doxology. These become, as common sense, universalising, that is, literalising devices through which language appears as both concrete and universal in its reference, in effect more real than real. Hence the literal exists as a placeholder with a universal capacity to equivalence particular terms via pseudo-articulations; it functions as an abstractional discursive reality.

Leaving aside for a moment the question of the literal as such 'false concreteness' it will be suggested here that two tropes of linguistic meaning; conventional/coded and living are necessary for communication and function interactively. Natural, everyday language functions as a contextual base for our identifications. It is as Russell (1973, pp.105, 108 f.2) argues essentially figurative, metaphorical. This nevertheless permits access to the topic of a situation because whilst the metaphor itself offers only indexical or indirect reference (contextual understanding), explicit identification is achieved from the way the figurative content is juxtaposed to conventional descriptions or names (Dummett, 1981) through which the utterance is objectified, classified.

Codes and context: Balzac

Michael Wood (2007, p.13) provides an illustration of this everyday process as presented in exemplary form in the work of Balzac. He does this through an account of the 'realism' of Balzac's descriptive technique. Now realism, as for the Symbolist Baudelaire, Wood argues, is equated with dead, literal textual accounts. However, Balzac's realism is different

...in the early pages of Le Père Goriot, Balzac describes, or keeps saying he can't describe the miserable Paris boarding house where much of the novel is set...

---

[54] That is to say, it has no reality (being) in everyday interaction but that it exists as a real abstraction in institutional discursive practice where it draws on living language, its trace, whilst displacing it, and functions there to equivalence or abstract concrete realities–see Chapter 1.

Writing like this is not a refusal of symbolism, it is a form of it, a selection of details to show what lies beyond the details. In the great works of Realism, surfaces always speak, they communicate with the depths the way a trapdoor communicates with a cellar or a space beneath a stage

Hence the details produce an epiphany; the things that Balzac refuses to name are 'metonymically named at once'. Balzac rejects didacticism; he does not say 'Madame Vauquer is the product of her environment' or that 'her house is a result of her personality'. The person, who is not approached directly, is equivalenced with the situating context and it is as such that we come to know Mme Vauquer, the landlady. The act of substitution, metonymy, tells us directly the truth of the situation. By not foregrounding the topic in its formal descriptive guise, as say, 'landlady of down-at-heel establishment', the accumulation of contextual detail provokes the denotative reference which identifies her in Wood's reading as 'someone who thrives off the misfortunes of others'. The substitution provides the force of the latter expression which could not be conveyed by the formal description in isolation. The content apprehended in a description is therefore unique, 'contextual', so that although it is done via a linguistic convention, for example 'landlady', what the formula of words actually refers to, denotes, is not conventional but 'situationally' unique. As Wood (loc. cit.) argues, 'this doesn't mean that context determines but rather that there is a correspondence between place and person and invites us to think of one in terms of the other'. We can see then that whilst the sense conveyed of the landlady is commonsensically thought to be reflected in what is asserted directly about her the fictive actuality of this person depends on the way formal description interacts with the taken for granted typifications used in a context which provides the range over which the conventional description articulates a particular field of objects/concepts and thus locates its actuality or sense, and thus it centrality or marginality to the field. This constitutes the semantic value or truth of the assertion, 'what has to be grasped to understand it' (Dummett, 1994, p.124, see also pp.24, 30, 125).

In phenomenological terms, then we might say that any communication, to be meaningful draws on the sedimented, 'lived' quality of the usage its discourse it 'brackets', or displaces. In other words, it is the usage through which it is articulated that denotes its object. It's the nature of this displacement which is relevant to issues around power, domination as can be shown from Wood's discussion of Balzac.

As Wood notes, the argument between Baudelaire and the Realists is about to what extent particular writing styles prove inspirational, evocative regarding their topic. It's clear that some writings are more evocative than others and here we can suggest that to the extent that writing remains within the realm of the conventional, formulaic, ossified or cliched then it fails to connect, to communicate a situation. The text is readerly, not writerly, to use Barthes' (2004, pp.4–11) terms, it dominates the reader rather than engaging the reader's own predicament. The reader's experience is not reflected in the text which rather, displaces the reader's engagement.

Barbaras (2006, p.55) casts some light on the phenomenology of this suppression of the subject from discourse. He argues that displacements can represent the original desire and projects in an idealised form in language or other objectifications (poems, letters, novels for example, H.F.) but that sometimes the objectifications fail to do this, in this case, engage readers. However, he goes on to argue, to maintain the reader illustration, the reader may associate their own sense of where the story should go with the text even though it actually doesn't do this. Rather than being in active engagement with the text the reader misrecognises it for what it displaces – their own sense of where it should go. Hence the text is invested with an import it does not possess and a desire that rightly belongs to a different, more writerly reading practice. [55] As Barbaras elaborates, what displaces the original under these circumstances is autonomous from it and hence nothing (non-being)[56] to it and so represents a lack or void in the reader's discourse, the other side of which is a misplaced concreteness, full presence, immediacy, a 'positivist' form of desire.[57] Because the subject still wants the object which has been displaced then it 'experiences the one that

---

[55] Debord (1983, 177) makes a related point about the temporal structure of the spectacle: the spectacle is a process in which fragments or sediments of past historical times reappear as seemingly autonomous elements of the present, as images which convey a misrecognition of the present. The traditional rural Gemeinschaft might be evoked in current urbanism garden cities and so on, but these lack the social relations of traditional communities. I owe this point to Evan Calder Williams.

[56] This is a radical form of non-being, 'pure nothingness' rather than an 'actual experience of lack or non-being at the very centre of presence' represented by the intentional context of an object (loc. cit.).

[57] Barbaras' critique of substitution in this positivistic mode is made in the context of Bergson's evolutionism where the substituting element (desire) is external to and autonomous from what it displaces.

replaces it as equivalent to nothing' in this situation. It is 'as if nothingness could exist only as totally opposed to being' rather than a lack which can be realised in the articulation of the subject within a determinate discourse.

Consequently, the attempt to equivalence the reader's desire with the readerly discourse by a kind of suture where autonomous abstractions are taken as a substitution for the subject's lived reality leads to misrecognition and radical dissatisfaction; the discreteness of the object of desire entails a form of pure nothingness, the (abstractional) object as ever-receding or 'being beyond itself'. Here the seduction of the surreal and its discursive politics is the other side of a radical lack, anxiety.

To put this in the frame of a living discursive practice, we turn to a phenomenology of language. Hence, whereas on the one hand, as Dummett (1981, p.30) argues, classification/coding is essential to linguistic practice:

> The use of language, if it is to have the point it is intended to have [reference-H.F.] must be a practice capable of being codified.

On the other, as indicated above, linguistic conventions, forms of descriptive classification do not themselves denote a reality, rather they mediate taken for granted or everyday typifications and usage and it is through this mediation that the actuality of texts/utterances is communicated.

> We must ask what makes the notion of a bearer of a name so transparent to us and why we accept. 'Aristotle' as standing for a man as unproblematic… |it| is embedded in very basic linguistic practices above all in the use of sentences where an object picked out by ostension [appeal to context-H.F.] is identified as the bearer of a name (ibid., pp.158–9).

Without the context principle (here 'context' entails the engagement of the reader) however, that is, in readerly mode, such mediating linguistic conventions or models can be mistaken for what they describe, as indicated by Baudelaire in his critique of bad, pedestrian, didactic realism (Wood, op. cit., p.13).[58] The possibility that this kind of misrecognition and substitution may be part of a repressive politics of communication is investigated below.

---

[58] This creates a false or misplaced concreteness where terms appear as autonomous and immediate rather than generated in a process of mediation. See also Chapter 1.

The notion of substitution rehearsed here can be contrasted with that offered by structuralism or post-structuralism. In our case, what is substituted, still impacts on what it is substituted for, maintaining a kind of fractured or decentred sense of structure. By comparison, the displacements of structuralism etc. take place absolutely in the sense that paradigms or even syntagms operate on a mutually exclusive basis (difference) rendering it impossible to think an idea outside the paradigm, for example. In the case of Foucault discourse, therefore appears as an overly deterministic mode of historical formation, what is excluded ceases to impinge on the discourse except as difference, what it is not. That is, what is excluded has no positive input, power to disrupt the discourse from within.

Ventriloquising the Everyday: The Literal as Hyperreal and Its Parallels with the Production of Value

It will be argued that the relationship between living language, ideology and power is akin to that which Arthur identifies between the commodity form of an object and its use value. Objects have a special kind of life once, as consumer goods they are inhabited by the commodity form, this misrepresents concrete use values in the guise of the hyperreal or false concreteness. In turn, the commodity depends for its 'life' on the concrete form of use value it displaces. In linguistic terms, the 'literal' also seems real and immediate because it inhabits the contextual reference (living language), context of signification in the way that the commodity inhabits concrete use values as a kind of absent presence or real abstraction. Arguably, the literal has likewise a reality conveyed by the abstractional processes of modern institutional life.

In Chapter 1, we looked at the literal or 'letter' as a way of repairing institutional/discursive crises, of renewing discursive practice by shifting the field of reference in which it operates. In this chapter, we can see the literal as functioning ideologically to suppress the shifts and insights that occur where there is a profound clash or void of meaning. The phenomenological Marxist insight here is that the literal derives its life from everyday, doxic practices which it then both displaces and impersonates as false or misplaced concreteness.

Moreover, the way it does this relies on the property of obviousness of the literal-conventional, its apparent power to define or 'label' the context. However, as argued in Chapter 1, the Duroux/Miller view of the literal ('letter') relies for its force, not on an intrinsic power to label situations but on its ability to articulate a trace or sediment, to link with the doxa of the culture and in this way to rejuvenate a signifying order or discourse Hence the displacement of the situation's trace in abstractional institutional practice makes the literal or formal institutional meaning look autonomous and under these conditions the abstract literal term 'floats free' as the placeholder or suture (see Chapter 1) and unites concrete aspects of discourse by equivalencing them. The act of equivalencing is potentially the weak point of the order of signification, the point where ambiguity or contradiction emerges. Hence, for example, 'labour' equivalences concrete and abstract labour; 'woman' equivalences sex and gender, and in both cases, as argued above, the tensions between different registers and their ontological implications emerge.

To return to the homology between the literal and the value form/commodification, as we have seen, in both cases forms of abstraction depend on something more concrete and more situated in lived experience as a vehicle for their resonance. At the same time, they displace this resonance into themselves thus enacting a kind of magic or ventriloquistic possession, a spectral presence. As Arthur notes,

> The spectre 'takes possession' of use value, estranges its meaning, drains away its truth, and substitutes a new one. Just as those possessed by spirits use their own larynx and tongue but speak in another voice, so use values are possessed by capital, in the spiritual as well as the legal sense (Arthur, 2001, p.40).

We can already see that this might have ideological implications when the production of language takes a bureaucratic or commodified form. The literal is itself situated by its context but the contextual trace/sediment is displaced in the peculiar economic and bureaucratic condition of modernity in an abstractional order of signification. As the literal, to pursue the analogy offered by Arthur, living language gains only the form of a phenomenal subject, its expressions are displaced into masks, personifications, in other words, typifications. Whilst in the case of capital, money not only 'stands for real wealth but elbows it aside and takes precedence' (ibid., p.41) in our case money is the equivalent of what might be called the currency of meaning, that is an autonomous and abstractional ('literal') language.

For Arthur (loc. cit.) in capitalism, money enters production and consumption as a spectre 'a secret subject, animating it, and vampire-like, communicating spectrality to all with which it has intercourse'. Under capitalism, 'the phenomenal subject is itself a spectre' (loc. cit.). This last point is crucial for the linguistic analogy. Through capital's inversion of the world of lived experience the ghost of the latter, if thought linguistically, is represented in the ossified forms of codified meaning and animates these forms with a false sense of immediacy. It is as if one could reach out and touch the generality of things, the 'sensuous supersensuous' (Marx, 1962, p.85) as with Baudrillard's (1999, p.328) account of ideology as hyperreality.

Althusser, Bourdieu, Foucault, Gramsci and Habermas have variously seen ideology as grounded in a genealogy of doxic elements and here we can see how the doxic might be mobilised as a cover or placeholder for ideology or in discourse, how a kind of ventriloquism temporalities is performed through which the doxic is enlisted in the service of institutional or state language.

The unspoken quality of the doxa of social practice, its indexical or 'natural' character constitute its everyday quality which *inter alia* Lefebvre (2002b, p.24) has identified with Merleau-Ponty's notion of lived experience. The institutional appropriations of the doxa produce a kind of inversion or 'rearticulation' of the everyday which reinforce the tendency towards inversion identified in phenomenological ontology where they characterise the 'being of the phenomenon' (Barbaras, 2004, passim). Here the transfer or disarticulation (epoché) of doxic content from a field of reference causes it to 'appear'; gives it a sense of immediacy where it is equated or synthesised with whatever generality is attempting to subsumed it (see Chapter 1). As Barbaras (2006, p. 80) notes, in the everyday world of 'the sensible', lived experience appears as both luminous and opaque, 'one experiences it simultaneously as evident and impenetrable' as immediate, and at the same time resistant to conceptualising subsumption. In the case of the literal, however, the transfer or inversion results in vacillations (hyperreal mimicry) rather than authentic rearticulations of the everyday and so it can be argued that the commodifying or reifying aspects of modernity amplify and colonise the experiential tensions within the everyday.

In linguistic terms, this can be elaborated as co-option by the literal whose immediacy then fails to deliver because it appears as both universal and concrete at the same time, as in fact, 'common sense', an unsituated interpellation of the subject's phenomenology. The literal remains an abstraction masquerading as 'the lived'. Lefebvre's (2002a, p.25) account of everyday life in the modern world also stresses this point and he notes (op. cit., pp.24-5) how the everyday both 'marks and masks', 'crowns and veils' the world of modern capitalism.

de Certeau: The Everyday as Appropriation and Metaphorisation

It can be seen from the above that in Lefebvre's account capitalist modernity both co-opts the everyday, becomes its inner spectre and is conversely also appropriated in the everyday as a transgressive or counter modernity: a kind of reverse colonisation or 'customisation' of modern capitalism occurs in everyday experience. The significance of Lefebvre's modern/everyday formulation here is that once transferred to the domain of communicative practice it establishes the ambiguity or vacillation of reference produced in the colonisation of language by formal systems of bureaucracy and commodity production. Hence Lefebvre's insights point to a structure of experience through which it is possible to reverse dominant meanings of ideology/discourse.

The work of Michel de Certeau (1988) exemplifies processes of appropriation in the everyday and this in turn recalls the discussion in Chapter 1 of the operationalisation of discourses and how, as Barthes notes, this requires a juxtaposition of the discourse, order of signification with the doxa of everyday life which in fact constitute the conditions of possibility (horizon) of the discourse as it gains its life through its articulation with/of the doxa. The corollary of this is that abstractions, discursive structures appear in doxic form. Here the discursive concept appears on the same level as the 'ordinary' that is, as part of its concrete, particular environment and thus its contextual relations and invisible potential are revealed. In Barthes' haiku model of understanding, the concept doesn't subsume the ordinary but rather, via a seism/*vaciller*, a synthesis takes place which shifts the field of perception/ reference. This is an actualisation of the concept's haecceity, its situation in the field of the doxa. In Chapter 1, it was further argued that such a move represents an equivocation within discourse, a suture[59] where its everyday conditions of possibility become evident and through which discourse can be operationalised via its articulation of the doxa.

de Certeau provides examples of such an operationalisation via his notion of the metaphorisation of formal systems to articulate the everyday of different

---

[59] 'suture' is used here in the Miller/Duroux sense of a placeholding signifier described in Chapter 1. However, it becomes clear that the suture also represents a colonisation, abstractional subsumption of the everyday. There are parallels with Lefebvre's everyday-modernity reversals here.

social groups which repairs the void in meaning for a given group. Metaphorisation is required in order to apply abstract/formal systems to real, concrete situations, to give them a sense of haecceity (A cognate idea in the work of symbolic interactionists such as Strauss (1964) is *negotiation* of formal systems). The other side of operationalisation is the rendering visible of suppressed aspects of discourse, the excess of meaning hidden or displaced in order to preserve its logical order or systematicity.

In the discussion of Balzac, we can see how the metaphor, as Wood (2007, p.13) notes, opens a perceptual 'trap door', once juxtaposed to the ordinary in the form of descriptive detail. Thus 'surfaces always speak'. This encounter, as with Barthes et al. moves us on, in its 'writerly' approach to the text, in enabling the reader to liberate hitherto invisible meanings in a situated appropriation of the text.

Metaphorisation is hence essentially processual or performative, it gives the meaning of the discourse etc. in the here and now. de Certeau's (1988, pp. 31–32) own examples involve the Spanish conquest of indigenous (S. American) Indian cultures, a project which 'was diverted from its intended aims by the use made of it'. The 'laws, practices and representations' imposed on them 'by force or fascination' were used 'to ends other than those of their conquerors' hence 'they subverted them from within'. They diverted the system towards 'rules, customs and convictions foreign to the colonisation…'. In other words, 'They metaphorised the dominant order: they made it function in another register. They diverted it without leaving it'. Elsewhere, de Certeau (op. cit., p.100) describes this diversion as from the 'faceless "proper" meaning', or 'literal', a 'normative' or idealised register of meaning. This functions as a placeholder, resolving contradictions between different discursive orders through enabling the doxa of a group to be articulated.

At the same time, as 'the literal' sutures such discursive orders to a dominant order, it masquerades as normative, or 'proper' and in this way dominant groups misrecognise their culture as *the* culture. (See also Bourdieu below). In this way it resembles abstractional displacement or equivalencing in that the proper or literal seems to equivalence different discursive orders through a signifier without determinate content. It entails ambiguous dispositions that divert and displace meaning in the direction of equivocalness in the way a tremulous image confuses the photographed object (loc. Cit.).

From the other angle, the dominant group's claim to the 'proper' colonises the subordinate groups in so far as the latter fail to recognise the invisible entailments of the suture and thus, as they must, remain within the suture of the dominant paradigm, as de Certeau (op. cit., p.32) notes.

At this point, we can move back to considering colonization, or inhabitation and appropriation, 'inversion' of the dominant order in Lefebvre's (2002a) wider context of modernity. As an articulation of the doxa, this duality or inversion of the social world can be seen as taking place *within* the everyday where capitalism might dominate this or might be subverted, appropriated as means of revolt against it (ibid., pp. 24–5).

The account of the spectrality of language above can, in different ways, be mapped onto the work of Habermas and Bourdieu. Habermas's 'colonisation of the lifeworld' is an argument about how the 'system world' occupies and as a hidden presence lives off the immediacy of the everyday communicative practice. Similarly, Bourdieu's discussion of delegated authority looks at the misrecognition of everyday action as a power removed to and resident in authorised language and ritual.

Misrecognition in the Social Theory of Habermas and Bourdieu

Habermas's theory of communicative action notes that formal systems remain parasitic on the everyday, lifeworld but not in any obvious way as in a traditional past marked by separate spheres of religious illusion which pass for the reality of everyday life. Rather contemporary parasitism takes the structures of the lifeworld itself and inhabits them as Habermas (1999) argues in his chapter 'Uncoupling of system and lifeworld'. The lifeworld is instrumentalised by system constraints that remain inconspicuous such that 'a communicatively structured lifeworld takes on the character of deception, of objectively false consciousness'.

The reproductive constraints that instrumentalise a lifeworld without weakening the illusion of its self-sufficiency have to hide, so to speak, in the pores of communicative action. This gives rise to a structural violence that without becoming manifest as such, takes hold of the forms of intersubjectivity of possible understanding [and]... is exercised by way of systemic restrictions on communication... the interrelation of the objective, social and subjective worlds gets prejudged for participants in a typical fashion (Habermas, 1999, p.174).

All the while, the systems world remains anchored in the lifeworld, its ontological base (ibid., p. 172). We don't have to agree with Habermas's taxonomy of social reality to take his point that typifications can be produced by modern capitalism and that they substitute themselves inconspicuously for interactions, practices, and so on, that appear self-sufficient and natural, that is, interactions which are taken for granted.

Thus the lifeworld is colonised, is taken over surreptitiously by the system which lives off it. Hence the lifeworld is hollowed out and becomes a sign for something else, state or capitalist practices masquerading as lifeworld.

Bourdieu

Bourdieu deals with the question of misrecognition as a process whereby one's own powers are misrecognised as those of instituted authority, an authority initially instituted by those (a social group) who now fail to recognise their action of delegation. Consequently, the powers of the institution are fed by the constituents who fail to recognise that these powers are constituted by their own actions (2006, pp.170–71). To put this another way, the official language is not recognised as having its source in the doxa of the everyday. Delegated authority acts as a kind of 'usurpatory ventriloquism' (1992, p. 211) and this applies to the dominant usage ('legitimate language') which is fiercely defended by subaltern groups as well as others. As Bourdieu says, there is a confusion of the idea of a common language with the actual usages employed by different social groups. Hence subaltern language users take the common language to be theirs in the sense of conveying their meanings but as Bourdieu (op. cit., p.54) points out legitimate language will convey dominant meanings, that is, communicate *its own meanings* through the 'common language'. [An example of this illusionary common is the obsession of the English middle classes with 'correct usage', etymology and so on]. Whilst Bourdieu is not so much concerned with the generation of meanings which function intersubjectively for and between social groups as with the production and reproduction of social difference through language, we will investigate the structures implicit in the idea of a common language and how this fetishistically comes to displace contextual meaning. Bourdieu is concerned with the differences between language users to the exclusion of group meanings which function through the common language in the sense that the latter inhabits and ventriloquises the former. His focus is on how the common language speaks for the subaltern groups rather than on how this acts as a vehicle of displacement for *their* meanings, that is, he doesn't pursue the fact that their delegated meanings still inform this fetishistic language, rather than the latter simply being a displacement *tout court* of, for example, popular meanings. In fact, Bourdieu's anaysis is oriented towards authority rather than meaning *per se*[60].

Nevertheless, the notion of a common language will be taken up below where Bourdieu's insight that authoritative speech depends on the ideological notion of a common language will be developed through an examination of 'the literal' in relation to power as manifest through a kind of linguistic displacement.

Language and power are not however to be equated Bourdieu argues in Language and Symbolic Power where he criticises Habermas for following Austin's notion of illocutionary utterance which does precisely this, that is, imbues words with power.

> He [Habermas-H.F.] thinks he has found in the specifically linguistic substance of speech the key to the efficacy of speech, one forgets that authority comes to language from the outside (ibid., pp. 107, 109).

This power, he argues, as with all symbolic ritual, stems from people themselves and is displaced via a process of misrecognition of the locus of power they have delegated to the ritual. Habermas's notion that communication produces social integration depends on the idea that language itself via common meanings has the power to produce consensus (Bourdieu, 1992, pp.107, 109). The rituals of conversation produce agreement once we have grasped the undistorted content. Here language is seen as an autonomous system of meaning much in the way that types/conventions come to be seen as autonomous vehicles

---

[60] Bourdieu deals with meaning crises in Outline, for example, but in terms of the unsayable becoming sayable, recognised, legitimate rather than of a group accessing its hidden historical legacy. See op. cit., pp. 168–171.

of meaning, a kind of hyperreality, as noted in the previous investigation of the literal and its substitution for the 'luminous/opaque' quality of the doxic.

Types, Barthes and Semiotic Closure

However, can this experiential structure of the doxic be applied to the already identified framework of communicative practice as domination? Arguably, the literal or readerly occupies the same ground as money in that both of these effect an equivalence between otherwise diverse concrete values (meanings, things). In other words, the literal functions in institutional settings as a real abstraction. Dummett's account of communicative practice enables us to separate out ordinary, living and dominative modes of communication, that is, to place the literal within the conceptual framework of communication developed here.[61]

By developing Dummett's approach, we can see the conventional description/name functioning in two ways: it can work as the representation of a communicative content via denoting or identifying a contextual meaning, alternatively it can function as 'the literal' where everyday typifications (living language) are transmuted into naturalised speech, the 'literally true'.

In the second guise, as the literal, conventional meaning works like money under the value form: literalisation transforms a relatively fixed level of meaning (conventional meaning) into something which displaces the multiple voices of a context of reading or speaking and achieves the status of a ghostly autonomy (naturalisation), the hyperreal (sensuous/supersensuous). As naturalised, it appears both as opaque and the flatly obvious, the taken for-granted of communication. Thus it 'speaks through' the sensuous as 'literal truth'. It is the reception of the taken for-granted as concrete, autonomous everyday life that lends its subversion by abstraction in the guise of sensuousness particular potency.

This readerly domination of the logic of communicative practice suggests that the everyday typifications of living language behind and informing the conventional descriptions with concrete meaning will in this case mask the conventional descriptions which crown them, following Lefebvre's stratagem. In other words, these will then via a reversal appear as what the convention identifies, denotes, that is, the concrete content. The mediator (conventional

---

[61] Dummett's truth conditional semantics distinguishes the meaning of linguistic conventions/codes from their contextual interpretation or 'sense'. See above.

term) becomes the mediated content, apparently an object in its own right. Conversely, 'objects' denoted in this way, people, things, consequently appear as types rather than individuated beings although they maintain the semblance of the sensuous via the living context upon which the literal/readerly is parasitic. For example, sociological models of class are sometimes read as representing autonomous concrete individual members.

It follows that what is subverted in the process of literalisation is not so much the object denoted in a communicative context but rather the relationship between the reference/identification and the way it is arrived at, the relationship between a process and its products or objectifications. As in the process of capitalist production, products appear as autonomous from their making and the process appears as contingent upon – mediated by – the product (Marx, 1974, p.76). The peculiar inversion is arguably consequent on the structure of experience engendered by the process of commodification.

Similarly, the linguistic everyday seems to be the outcome or objectification of communication rather than the generating process; it is silenced, masked as the object denoted. Consequently, the literal represents an oscillation or *vaciller* between generating ground and its object, living language and its conventional abstraction, each takes on features of the other, that is, each masks the other but the latter dominates (Lefebvre, op. cit., pp.24–25). Thus the identifications in communicative practice appear also as their everyday typifications/generating ground and so take on the hue of natural, autonomous existents. As Barthes (2004, pp.16, 23) argues, texts become essentialised and naturalised, rendered univocal as connotations are silenced via the 'naturalisation of their production'. For Barthes (op. cit., p.9), conventional descriptions ('denotations' in the parlance of semiotics) equivalence, sum up, serve as a common denominator of a field of connotations. They are in fact themselves connotations but the ideological (illusional) process of literalisation, renders them primordial. Hence the concluding connotative utterance serves to structure and render the polyvocity of the rest which the concluding term now equivalences, invisible. The readerly text or reading has the feel of concrete, spontaneous communication, the immediacy of descriptive prose, that is, it condenses the meaning of what's gone before into itself in its now-literal function. This is the false or misplaced concreteness of the sensuous-supersensuous, the suture or connection that is a disconnection. As the non-being of the literal the concreteness of connotation masks the conventional description, implying the obvious, commonsense immediacy of the readerly. There is no perceived separation of concrete and conventional meanings and as such the structure of perception is radically altered towards textual closure and the authoritative reading. One might, for example, think of a media discussion in which people's access to markets is defined abstractly in terms of the choices they make, regardless of their financial circumstances or actual desires, tastes. Their choices seem to be concrete, personal but in reality, they're informed by abstractions of/from economic and cultural situatedness. A further discussion of the readerly and its institutional foundations is found below.

Labelling and identity

A key implication of this account of the readerly text is that it breaks with the commonsense and mistaken view of linguistic domination as labelling, the generally accepted account of stereotyping. It does this by showing how a concrete, lived content rather than purely discursive description functions in the dissemination of power. The social constructionist account of linguistic power, on the other hand, works from a fetishistic understanding of the power of definitions, and so on, rather than integrating domination by labelling into a spectral ontology of the literal as living language, as is arguably demonstrated here. The reality of the readerly as spectral presence is demonstrated in the way identities are shaped. In Fanon's *Black Skins White Masks,* individuals are ideologically interpellated as the colonial subject inhabiting a lived identity, for instance. The individual is picked out both as individual and a type; one masks and naturalises the other. The subject thus appears as hyperreal in the trappings of essential 'Africanness', 'negritude' etc. (Fanon, op. cit., pp.92–5, 97). Regardless of whether this is valued positively or negatively it forms a barrier to self-actualisation, somatic violence is done by splitting the colonial subject from its lived experience whilst at the same time the dominant discourse inhabits and lives off the former as an essentialised identity.

The Readerly and Its Metaphorical Subversion: Barthes, Lefebvre, Balzac

In Barthes' *S/Z* texts are essentially performative, in-process, a coming-to-be, and as productions of the reader, metaphorical work (p.213). The politics of reading is mediated through connotative fields generated through textual production where semantic closure (literalisation), is contested (ibid., pp.8–9).

This still seems to leave us without a principle of ideology critique though. That is, what ontology allows us to contest the bureaucratisation of reading, how can we make sense of the materiality of these linguistic tendencies? As Lefebvre (2002a, p.32) argues, if we are to understand the contestation and reversibility of signification then we must grasp that it is grounded in the everyday: the everydayness of any topic, the open-endedness of the routine structure through which it is apprehended, allows this switch of perspective. In other words, predication or signification is a translation which applies a routine or ordinary, generic action, commentary, to a particular thing, the topic or signified[62]. Essentially then, the bureaucratic or rationalised character of modernity is grounded in the everyday, with which it maintains an interdependent relationship (ibid., p.24), a point further elaborated in the next section. To continue, before we develop the everyday/modernity distinction, he argues, '…there is nothing but aimless signifiers and disconnected signifieds. You are led astray by mirages when you try to connect a signifier to a signified' (ibid., p.25). However, given the distinction between the 'two interdependent realities', modernity and everyday life, 'you are now the active interpreter of signs'. In fact, '…both sides signify each other reciprocally; each one in turn becomes a signifier or signified according to slant of the enquiry' (loc. cit.). The reversibility of signification thus opens up a critical leverage which uses the everyday as its ground.

This insight into the *translatability* of signification according to situation or social world is also crucial to Wood's discussion of Balzac's realism (see above) where Wood (loc. cit.) observes, his style 'asserts a correspondence between place and person and invites us to think of one in terms of the other'. Hence Balzac's realism not only offers 'a profusion of material signs but also leads to a theory of the readability of those signs'. There is a metonymic relationship in *Le Pére Goriot* between for example, Mme Vauquer, the landlady and her circumstances.

Her whole person explains the boarding house, just as the boarding house implies her person [*toute sa personne explique la pension, comme la pension implique sa personne*] (loc. cit.).

The juxtaposition of a description which 'explains' and the personage of the landlady enables ('implies') a metaphorical transfer or realisation of Mme

Vauquer as a subject/topic of the text. In his way, the signifier/signified reversal or *vaciller* releases new or hidden meanings.

The equivalencing of landlady and boarding house leaves open the intentionality of the text, one term does not dominate the other but leaves open the possibility of multiple readings of the factors relating to the trajectory of an individual in a specific socio-historical context.

Lukács' (1971, pp.108–9) insights on Balzac are useful here. He notes that what enriches Balzac's texts is the interplay between complex plot, diverse individual trajectories against a background of homogenisation of his characters' worldviews.

> The outside world is essentially peopled by human beings with similar mental structures although with completely different orientations, we [thus] obtain that strange immeasurable mass of interweaving destinies and lonely souls...

Hence the psychology of the landlady implies a certain conventionalisation of personality but this is offset by the sheer unpredictability of her trajectory which implies vis á vis the reader an engaging, writerly relation to the text.

This textual polivocity means we can then start from the fact that the depressing room which 'exhales an odour...stuffy, musty and rancid...[whilst] The panelled walls...once painted some colour...now...[are] encrusted with accumulated layers of grimy deposit' (Balzac cited loc. cit.) stands in for the trade of the landlady which is largely in the misfortune of others (from which she benefits) or take the encapsulation of Mme Vauquer, 'sleek as a church rat' as a metonym for her trade, and so on. It is clear then that the functioning of the metonym depends on the conventional understanding and vice versa in these images of the landlady's trade/persona and that this reciprocal relation or *vaciller* enables a reversal of perspective, translation of the text to new fields of reference, new ways of articulating the reading subject.

However, the trope of textual closure is the predominant tendency of modernity as Lefebvre argues. He associates modernity with the acceleration of codification. A signal or code differs from the symbol or sign

> in that its only significance is conventional, assigned by mutual agreement; in this respect it can be compared to certain signs such as letters that compose

articulated units (words and monomials) but that are otherwise meaningless... signals can be grouped as codes (The highway code is a simple and familiar example), thus forming a system of compulsion... Signals and codes provide practical systems for the manipulation of people and things (op. cit., p.62).

Barthes (2004, p.4) has similarly argued that the reduction of communication to monovocal or readerly texts is a way of depriving the reader of agency: that the denotative description/definition of a context is way of closing down the plurality of a text and the reader's interpretive agency:

Our literature is characterised by the pitiless divorce which the literary institution maintains between the producer and the text, between its owner and its customer, between author and reader.

And on another level such institutional abstraction means that 'denotation', the conventional, definitional, taken *tout court,* closes down textual polyvalence.

Ideologically, [denotation]...has the advantage of affording the classic text a certain innocence...It is ultimately no more than the last of the connotations (the one that seems both to establish and close the reading)... language as nature...something simple, literal, primitive (ibid., p.9).

Arguably, this line of thought can be extended to cover the abstractional implications of such institutional equivalencing and closure of textual production, the 'canonical', and so on, along the lines developed above in Chapters 1 and 2.[62]

---

[62] Whilst translation or metaphoric transfer indicates a differentiation it also contains a resembling moment. In phenomenological terms this represents a continuity, an open horizon of typical familiarity, its everyday (see Schutz, 1967, pp.7-8).
Davies (1989) provides a useful account of institutional appropriation of writing in the 19th century U.K. where 'the literary', the canon and so on is coproduced by the need for a pedagogy that provides a literary ideology to give an imaginary resolution 'as Macherey puts it' to the class contradictions of the national social formation (op. cit., pp.253 - 4).

A recent example of resistance to this appropriation of the living practices of reading was the refusal of the 2019 Booker Prize jury to rank the 'top' entries.

Davies (1989) provides a useful account of institutional appropriation of writing in the 19th century U.K. where 'the literary', the canon, and so on, is coproduced by the need for a pedagogy that provides a literary ideology to give an imaginary resolution 'as Macherey puts it' to the class contradictions of the national social formation (op. cit., pp.253–4).

Another example of this trope of discursive closure, where signification or reading is annexed to a dominant discourse, discussed in Chapter 3, is where the topic or paradigm of 'health and fitness' is displaced/subsumed via the commodified language of 'health and beauty'. Here, the idea of getting fit is annexed to that of shape, which becomes the placeholder, and along the way a whole field of connotations is assimilated to this purpose. 'Shaping up', 'getting into shape', being in good shape – and by extending the metaphor of shape, 'a fit woman' (*sic*) – are some of the meanings which can be used to bolster this new (sexist) articulation. This moves the emphasis from 'health' to 'beauty' and in effect seals off, sutures the meaning of getting fit from lived experience of exercise and health, whilst continuing to trade off its echoes, to speak through ventriloquise, the doxa of fitness. Displaced 'fitness' although opaque, a void or non-being in discourse, is therefore nonetheless, a spectral presence. Its lack becomes a source of anxiety in perpetually threatening to break through into luminous reality, to demand more than can be said – and in this way the commodified nature of such discourse produces radical dissatisfaction. The desiring subject of this discourse experiences lack as the 'perpetual being beyond itself'. Here the literal or placeholder, 'shaping up' and so on, carries with it the anxiety of repressed meaning/subjectivity and 'conveys' its trace in a way that denies its actual expression. This anxiety and its expression in the form of phantasy objects such as stereotypes is discussed elsewhere in the text.

Deconstructing the Concept: Surplus Without Expropriation? The Everyday as Critical Residuum

As we've already seen here, if we lose sight of fitness as a process, a translation drawing on the doxa or everyday of the term, then its signification becomes arbitrary and an abstractional placeholder for commodified equivalencing. It is however important to investigate whether the abstraction of process, the displacement of the metaphoricity of fitness, and so on, inevitably results in the commodification of linguistic practices. The question, to paraphrase Ricoeur (see below), is: 'how does conceptualisation, as abstraction, relate to its conditions of possibility, its metaphorical grounds?'

If we take the example 'spending time', then on the face of it, there seems to be nothing of the synecdoche here, no part-whole relation, its meaning is flat, obvious. On the contrary, once the two terms are unpacked we can see that spending is about using up money and time is often equated with money, time as a commodity – labour time. Hence both terms are in possession of the logical equipment to produce the metaphorical affinity/relation. In performing this operation, we are enlivening the sedimented logics in speech, bringing to mind what actually goes on all the time anyway. As Derrida (Ricoeur, 1986, p.286) argues, 'language works behind our backs' and metaphor is a sort of 'linguistic surplus value'. Ricoeur (op. cit., p.284) comments that this functions

unknown to speakers, in a manner in which in the economic field the product of human labour is made at once unrecognisable and transcendent in economic surplus value and the fetishism of merchandise.

As such, 'spending time' is a dead metaphor, the result of a wearing a way of meaning (*usure*) through which the metaphor is 'raised' to the status of concept, as Hegel argues (ibid., p.286). Derrida's deconstruction thus unmasks the concept, revealing its metaphysical presuppositions, its trace. Conversely, the concept bereft of it trace in the sensible world appears as an idealisation with all the dualistic problems that raises about, for example, the nature/culture relation, as explored in Chapter 2 via the sex/gender dualism. This binary classification, it was argued, results from the divorce of sex/gender from its basis in the everyday notion of 'woman' – a way of mediating, grounding these abstractions. Two questions are prompted by Ricoeur's discussion. Firstly, is *usure* the same as commodification, which Ricoeur asserts here, that is, does it operate not only as a parallel or analogy but is it the same sort of process? Secondly, what is the status of the trace or sediment provided by *usure* in Derrida, can it operate as a means of demystification in the way that we have looked at the doxa as a criterion for unmasking abstraction?

Arguably, the answer to the first question is 'no'. The reason for this is that *usure* is an abstraction or conventionalisation which when situated by metaphorical process can result in a translation where the meaning of the abstraction is realised in a different field of reference. In other words, the reference of the abstraction is actualised by the situating metaphor, as in the case of Wood's account of metonymy in Balzac. By contrast, Ricoeur notes Hegel as seeing the conceptual abstraction as divorced from the situating content it subsumes. In other words, negation of the negation or subsumption (*Aufhebung*) leaves no actual or relational remainder.

However, ironically, a similar move is made by Ricoeur (op. cit. pp.300-301), when he notes that theoretical or 'speculative' abstractions are divorced from the lived or doxa, 'perception or images', which was their ground; a form of epistemological break. This mode of analysis is also found in structuralist thinkers such as Bourdieu (2006, p.9) and Althusser (1977, pp.35–6), who sever science from the everyday, with the consequence that reference is divorced from context in which it is made, with all the problems of circularity, closure or hermeticism this raises. Hence we can conclude that abstraction is divorced from metaphorical process in these thinkers.

Abstraction and the actuality of modernity

Hegel's identification of abstractions that subsume their grounds, that is, with no concrete content is however a perception based on the actuality of modernity. In the *Philosophy of Right*, money equivalences the services provided by the modern state. This instantiate real relations with no determinate content, which function to externally equivalence concrete entities in a way which is arbitrary in that it ignores the concrete relations between actual entities (Hegel, 1942, pp.623, 194). Now the process of *usure* does not necessarily involve this 'extreme' form of 'externality', that is, its abstractions may have quite concrete implications which are realisable via a re-enlivening of their 'dead metaphors' which hence provide an opening or articulation for the subject within a discourse.

As argued above, real abstractions are not simply external to concrete things but come to inhabit them as evidenced in equivocations or vacillations between concrete things and the abstraction itself. These form a spectral presence in the lived quality of the doxic or every day. In terms of signification, it was suggested that such equivocations are semiotically represented as abstractional placeholders, sustaining the weak or critical point in a discursive practice, the region of *basculer* (Duroux, 2012b, pp.187, 190) or overturning of the signifying order.[63]

---

[63] Such placeholders gain a cultural purchase, a partial interpellation of subjects, through

This abstractional form of displacement, as McNulty (2012b, pp.92–3) argues, is ideological in that it involves a misrecognition, a repression of the subject from discourse. A crisis of signification is hence 'solved' by a kind of impersonation or ventriloquism where an object or term is displaced (substituted), as both Arthur (2001, pp.36, 40) and Barbaras (2006, p.55) have noted in their own ways.

The substitution is experienced as nothing to what is displaced creating a void or radical sense of dissatisfaction where the displaced or doxic appears as an equivocation (*vaciller*)[64] of the experiential with the signifying abstraction.[64] Hence, as Duroux (op. cit., p.190, n.6) suggests the doxic appears not only as particular but as a kind of general particular, something quite transcendental and autonomous, in fact as the hyperreal, as it suffuses the abstraction which in turn presents it as a universal, as a fully present, immediate reality. The equivocation also represents a hiatus in discourse and it is clear from both Duroux (op. cit., p.193) and McNulty (loc. cit.) that this void intimates the return of the repressed, it is a space within which the subject can be interpellated differently, find discursive expression, despite the seductions of the abstraction and its effects on the agent's desires via the hyperreal.

The void or nothing of signification, as Duroux and Miller have argued, is in fact the constitutive outside of signification, the context in which identifications are forged and where signification is contested; it is where *vaciller* can result in the transfer of signifiers from one field of reference to another. Hence, it is a site where the lived world can be reappropriated as Sandford (see Chapter 2) in effect argued in relation to the doxa of lived sexuality and its mobilisation against institutional appropriation as an abstraction in the form of sex hierarchy.

Abstract, arbitrary equivalencing was also a feature of Wood's discussion of Balzac where the bad, one-dimensional readerly realism of the 19th Century

---

the lived appropriation of abstractional content within the overall framework of subsumption it imposes as with the Amerindians' appropriation of forms of Christianity within the colonial context, as de Certeau's (1984) above case study shows.

[64] Vaciller represents the moment in which the sediment/trace or doxa is in transition to a new field of reference and thus as it is freed from its signifying order appears as immediate, obvious, common sense. Where it is appropriated by real abstractions, however, vaciller continues as here there is no synthesis with a new field of reference. This is experienced as radical dissatisfaction and its correlative – seductive unmediated desire of the (narcissistic) self-identical subject.

novel is more than a problem of *usure* and rather one of real abstraction and its suture. Here the relation of metaphor to the concept is one which renders the former's content arbitrary in relation to its living context. The designated readerly, literal meanings, the result of the impact of abstraction on reading practices can be seen in cases where the literal/readerly masquerades as the sensuous, for example, even in literary theory/criticism the critic informs us of the immediacy of the language of a text whilst at the same time interpreting that 'natural' implication, thus, ironically, imposing a reading, that is, offering a readerly text. The displaced significations or 'surplus value' of the text mask the atrophy performed by the readerly. As suggested above Dummett's emphasis on the interaction between (conventional) text and context, that genuinely refers, incorporates the reader's experience, and thereby offers an antidote to this. By contrast, the sutured textual practice, as McNulty (loc. cit.) notes, represses the subject from discourse.

Abstraction, signification and the everyday

Arguably then, the elective affinities between alienating/repressive abstractions of state and capitalism indicated by Hegel and others[65] have implications for situating the readerly. Because the equivalencing functions of property relations, contractualism of buying and selling in markets, (abstract) individualisation by state and market, and so on, issue in the rule of formal institutional codes and languages the genesis of the readerly should not be seen as a separate process from capitalist modernisation but rather as a feature of it. The intertwining of commodification and formal institutional relations can be seen through the notion of exchange which appears, in a perspectival switch or translation, both as economic – the realisation of value, and at the same time, a legal-contractual relation between buyers and sellers. Both of these aspects of abstraction circulate and regulate systemically, and here exchange is at the same time subsumption. Signification is therefore sutured, closed; a language that comes to us from 'the outside', a kind of 'commodity language'.

Hence commodification of language, the masking of its surplus of meaning, is just part of the abstractional process that prevails particularly in the sphere of

---

[65] Halewood (2013, p.160) has noted the mutually reinforcing processes of individualisation in state and market, for instance. See also Bhandar and Toscano (2015, p.9) on Marx's use of the Hegelian formulation of property as abstractional displacement in characterising capitalism.

consumption (see discussion of the everyday in the section on Lefebvre: the everyday as masking commodification).[66] It follows that the spectre or abstraction feeds off the linguistic surplus in relation to the production and realisation of value because signification here is a process related to accumulation.

Lefebvre (op. cit., p.32) observes that signification, as culture, is necessarily 'inherent in a mode of existence', ideologies pursue an active role. The everyday, routine or *usure* as an aspect of communication appears inhabited by capitalist modernity (and in turn, as a more subversive phenomenon, appropriates and recreates modernity).

The former receives attention from Lefebvre (loc. cit.) when he notes that class interests 'cannot ensure the totality of a society's operative existence unaided'. The everyday provides, as excluded residuum, the determinate totalising moment in an otherwise fragmented social field of 'all the specific and specialised activities outside social experience',[67] as such it is 'the sociological point of feedback' (loc. cit.). Therefore as well as being the standpoint of critique, interruption of closed, commodified signification it is also arguably, a reproductive site, the 'operative' moment in which capitalism is organised, metaphorised; this is the point at which the spectre is made 'flesh', value is created and living labour is colonised.

The open text

The second question raised about the silent linguistic surplus, 'does the trace in Derrida provide a way of linking the routine content of language to abstractions in an open-ended interactional way?' is in effect answered by reference to the above. Derrida's rejection of phenomenology and his absolutisation of absence in relation to presence (Derrida, 1982, p.43, Wood, 1989, p.271) suggests not, and as we've seen from Lefebvre the everyday entails this very intertwining of absence and presence. Derrida's (Ricoeur, op. cit., p.286) account of *usure* whilst noting a passing into routine of metaphor cleaves

---

[66] See also Khatib (2017, passim) on the commodification of language as a form of real abstraction.

[67] In the everyday, abstractional divisions and hierarchies are perceived as continuities within a situated horizonal perspective, relations rather than separate categories. Hence, they are not experienced as abstractions. Lefebvre (2002b, p.24) acknowledges his debt to Merleau-Ponty (the notions of lifeworld and lived experience).

this from the concept produced in this process of conventionalisation. This contrast with the metonymic process in the Balzac illustration where metaphor depends on conventionalisation ('the landlady'), part substituted for whole and vice versa: context and topic are intertwined not sub/superordinated, indicating the polyvocity of the text. The personality of the landlady, Mme Vauquer, communicates the social situation and reciprocally, the situation gives us the psychology of Mme Vauquer. As Waldron (1967, p. 162) has argued, the opening of a text, the metaphoric transfer, occurs when one takes say, 'the landlady' as conventional, ordinary meaning and juxtaposes this to her (explanatory) context.

To characterise this phenomenologically, it can be argued that one term is taken for granted, routinised in relation to the other, one becomes the background or contextualisation of the other (foregrounded as topic, figure). This moment can be reversed; background becomes foreground, topic is 'reduced' to context. Balzac's writing in effect facilitates reversal because his realism promotes a constructed polivocity or openness of the text. Here arguably the reader provides elements of background which enter into debate with the intentionality of textual reception practices, the conventions of 'Balzac reading' and so the open text promotes a fusion with the reader's perspective rather than its resisting equivocation as with Barthes' 'readerly text'.

Hence it can be seen from Balzac that reversals of perspective are a way of appropriating the descriptive, explanatory abstraction, as Barthes indicates via his haiku stratagem (see in Chapter 1). Here the ordinary, conventional and its invisible doxic basis, a result of *usure*, the wearing-away, connects with its predicate through a situated reading. In this way, the textual reversal allows for a shift in perspective, which creates an opening, 'asserts a correspondence between place and person and invites us to think of one thing terms of the other'. Such a *Gestalt* switch enables the reader to see person and place as situated in a horizon of possibility of each other, as a moment of resemblance and synthesis of metaphorisation.

Displacement as synthesis and polivocity

The relation between the metaphoric and the everyday becomes clear: they both represent a continuum of perception, a totalising moment in which the elements or signs are seen as configured by their conditions of possibility rather than abstractional subsumption.

This openness is, in other words, an interruption of Barthes' explanatory or syllogistic tendency, a way of thinking the text as dialogue with the reader, it allows the reader to translate or articulate their lived discursivity or subjectivity with the text, via the 'trap-door' moment (*vaciller*) noted above.

Hence this seism or metonymic shift indicates a potential switch of perspective, via a fusion or synthesis of genus and species in a different way, indicating the particularity of the general and the generality of the particular. The boarding house becomes more landlady-like and vice versa; each is seen as a moment of the other; an event in which new conceptual possibilities are intimated metaphorically.[68]

Whilst the metonymic relation (metaphorisation) represents a reversal of the topic, as with of place/person in the above, Ricoeur (op. cit., p.197, Feather, op. cit., p.76) notes, as previously indicated, that it also involves a moment of connection or resemblance to what is displaced, and so there is no subsumption (translation) without remainder in the sense of Hegel's *Aufhebung*.

> Can one not say that the strategy of language at work in metaphor consists in obliterating the logical and established frontiers of language, in order to bring to light new resemblances the previous classification kept us from seeing? In other words, the power of metaphor is to establish new logical frontiers on the ruins of their forerunners.

From a phenomenological perspective, Barbaras has argued, in a way sympathetic to the above discussion that there is, beyond any defining description also a co-existing 'concrete negative'[69] or critical everyday 'presence' through which a transfer of meaning can be effected. This concrete of the everyday has only a spectral presence in commodified discourse but, as Lefebvre shows, within the everyday itself as a totalising residuum of modern capitalism, even such discourse is open to what it excludes, becomes particular rather than purely abstractional, exists on a continuum with/as the ordinary or doxic. This appropriation of formal systems is achieved discursively, following de Certeau, through metaphorisation, the particularising effects of performativity,

---

[68] Waldron (op. cit., p.162), for example, notes Aristotle's insight on metaphoric transfer as metonym or synecdoche.

[69] A horizon within which the object moves and is under on-going constitution, as Barbaras (2006, p.125) characterises this aspect of being.

the way the discourse is operationalised within a specific context (thus revealing its haecceity).

Whilst both de Certeau and Lefebvre point to appropriations of modernity within the everyday, we have looked at the question of how such *Gestalt* or seism might be translated such that modernity itself might be capable of new, non-abstractional social worlds. Abstractional discourses resist such translations as arguably illustrated by the phenomenon of unresolved *vaciller*, which indicates the suppression of the subject from discourse.[70]Commodified language, discourse it has been argued, therefore represents a special case of abstraction, that of *real* abstraction.

However, even when the translation of the subject to new socio-linguistic worlds, fields of reference is achieved the truth of its concepts can only be maintained where it continues to be viewed in its making, as a process, that is synchronic with its cognitive outcome; that is, as metaphor and coincidentally its conceptual product. The occulted or auratic dimension of the outcome is hence tangible, connects with the living subject. Such a moment is suggested above in the Balzac illustration.

Translation thus constitutes a moment of reflexivity in which the coming to be and destination are held simultaneously by the subject, as a state of affairs akin to Keats' idea of metaphoric 'negative capability' (Smith, 2009, p.145–7). Here 'equivocation' is sited in a 'voice [that] relinquishes ownership of itself, develops a creative sense of dissociation' (ibid., p.147). This subject has 'simultaneous truths' (ibid. p.145), is an 'irreducible multiplicity' [of identities] whose contradictions pull the subject into different trajectories, horizons, projects.

Again, in phenomenology this sense of reversibility, ambiguity or equivocation is noted by Merleau-Ponty (1992, pp. 94–5) through the notion of a hyperdialectic. Here, subjectivity, the 'thetic' or 'idealisation' is thrown into relation with itself as it is constituted by its social situation, forcing it to confront the objectivity within itself, the juncture of the 'in-itself and for-itself' as the site

---

[70] This is the subject's concrete content appropriated previously that masks the abstraction's arbitrariness, its formal, literal, faceless character as definitive of commodification or bureaucratic rationalisation. On the other hand, within the everyday, the latter 'unravels' as its doxic form – as 'labyrinthine', 'faceless bureaucracy' and so on, that is, as subject to the critique of everyday life.

of the 'there is something', that is, of actualisation. In this metaphoric transfer, subsumption (*Aufhebung*) is 'partial, encumbered with survivals'.

Whilst, as we can see, different terms, positions coexist within communication how they are *read*, as suggested in the above discussion will depend on a 'politics' of communication, the capacity of readers to adopt a position both within and beyond a discursive practice in order to decode the signs and contest ideological displacements, the suturing of meaning in modernity.

5

Cracking Capitalism...

The network of interdependencies amongst human beings is what binds them together...a structure of mutually oriented and dependent people. It expresses what we call 'society' as neither an abstraction of attributes of individuals nor a 'system' or 'totality' beyond individuals but rather a network. (Elias, 2000, p.261)

Where Are the Cracks[71]?

The recent focus on networking as a means to personal success may be no more than the sensing of an epiphenomenon, an echoing of an everyday reality, the spectral presence of capital in what we take to be spontaneous contacts on the Internet etc. However, the business-speak *de nos jours* (cf. J. Hobsbawm on networking[72]) may also be an indicator of something profoundly central to capitalist modernity: something lateral that escapes hierarchy, subsumption, subjection to formations of capital.[73] The modus operandi of student protest, the Occupy movement, for example suggests a form of networking that evades commodification. The concern of this discussion is with the way the coordination and reciprocation constitutive of networks gets subsumed within modern capitalist social formations and the potential for circumventing this subsumption

---

[71] This discussion was provoked or stimulated by reading Holloway's Crack Capitalism. The piece is not a response to Holloway and interprets cracks not as alternative spaces but as something more dynamic, conflictual representing not just escape routes, but rather a systemic intertwining of different forces which open up lines of visibility.

[72] Hobsbawm (2012), p.43.

[73] See Harvey (2012), Rebel Cities: From the Right to the City to the Urban Revolution, for a critique of 'horizontalism', the pitfalls of which, hopefully, this chapter avoids.

of the visible cracks, the tensions within the everyday life of capitalism. The chapter is a survey of some ideas that might facilitate seeing through or around modern capitalism.

Giddens and Mouzelis: Structuration Theory

The way into this discussion is made via a detour into the exchange engendered over the existence of hierarchy and networks by Giddens' structuration theory.

Mouzelis (1995, pp.123–4) points out that Giddens in his theory of duality of structures does not deal with hierarchy although referring to power as a resource in relation to legitimacy. The implication here then is that this is a 'flat' theory rather than a theory of stratification, a theory of 'interconnection'. On the other hand, Mouzelis, through his metaphorical image of a dualism of interaction and structure[74] falls prey to the polar opposite position by absolutising the difference between formal hierarchies which have structural properties and other features of social life which don't; structure and hierarchy are elided here, giving the sense that, for example, network-type relations don't have structural properties.

Arguably, every hierarchy is also a network in which stratification is grounded: the members of hierarchies relate to each other as *interactants*, as elements of a network, as rhizomes, as well as rank statuses etc.

How do we know this? As Giddens (2001) points out, in a Heideggerian gesture, we bring to our interactions the whole of our experience, sedimented then activated by situation. It's not systematised but yet structured by the way it's laid down, so one thing evokes another by association. It's differentiated by the way it's activated according to the requirements of time and place. As such, we as embodied beings represent a historical trajectory and biography, including that of others, past struggles, outcomes. In this sense, all are represented, regardless of rank, in an agent's doings. All this is translated when an agent acts; not that an agent is necessarily capable of drawing consciously on all that they set in motion, all that they metaphorise, condense within their actions. Nevertheless, they draw on the accumulated experience of their interactions and those of others, on other times and places without recourse to differentiation or

---

[74] Mouzelis characterises the distinction above as one of syntagm (interaction) and paradigm (positioning of the former in social hierarchies). See Parker (2000, pp.94–6).

classification as what they mobilise is a continuous stream of contingent, historically episodic, occasional content, the doxa of practice (see Gramsci, Bourdieu, Foucault for instance).

This flow of associations gets organised, articulated via discourses, ideologies which configure its directionality, politico-cultural impact, effecting semantic closure. Consequently, the political impact of the organisation of cultural products/associations is to render them less accessible, visible.

Any scheme or project acknowledges the cultural associations it organises and internalises at the same time as it negates, displaces this content. The bracketed/black-boxed content lives on as the conditions of possibility of that which bracketed it: whatever is displaced here in turn mediates its successor. As such it is an absent presence as Giddens (op. cit., pp.78, 141-2) remarks in relation to his notion of time-space distantiation; it's there but not there, a positive content given to us through whatever directly confronts us.

Giddens conveys a sense of how things are interconnected or networked where networks appear as a kind of punctualised, displaced penumbra of interrelations behind any specific encounter, engagement. Networks stand behind agents as a resource for the latter. However, Giddens, like Goffman (Mouzelis, op. cit., p.107) does not confront the hierarchisation implicit in discursive organisation of social interrelations and so it's hard to see how agents are situated by power structures; agents always appear as interacting *sembables*[75] rather than carriers of an institutional order which situates them in power relations.

Clearly (with Mouzelis) hierarchy is real but at the same time it is abstract; it posits relationships which exist outside the way people relate spontaneously beyond the bureaucratic definitions and requirements of formal settings; in that sense it is a reorganisation of concrete, informal relationships, ways of doing. As such, it is a mode of abstraction from interactions as networks of associations where their shifting nodal points are appropriated and filtered through hierarchies of power and status. The power of galleries and the music industry over artists are obvious cases in point. It is thus suggested that formal contractual organisations are derivative of the spontaneous, lived relations they subsume.

---

[75] Equals, neighbours, colleagues. A 'plurality of beings' whose trajectories overlap 'even when some seek to enslave others' and whose common situation means that 'adversaries are often in a kind of complicity'. Difference undergoes a kind of suspension. See Merleau-Ponty (1991a, p.10)

That is, networks are the ontological ground of formal institutions because they already contain the (non-abstractional) content which appears as re-figured in hierarchisation, where nothing lived, concrete is added to the already existing relations.

It is this subsumptive dualistic character of formal contractual social relations – at once lived and abstractional – that Marx *inter alia* identifies in production and exchange relations in modern capitalism. 'Labour' as Marx (1974, p.78) argues has a 'two-fold social character': the shape the value of commodities takes ultimately depends on 'living labour', the concrete relationships between producers, producers and products and producers and capitalists. Use value is open-ended and depends on specific contexts and so commodities are shaped by creative forces outside the generality of the value form and carry this with them to be extracted in different ways by different concrete users.

We can think of this working in a similar way to that in which language once freed from the dead hand of a fetishistic literal or readerly usage is capable of generating multiple meanings for different users. By contrast, abstraction can be likened to the subsumption of the metonymic (figures of speech) as conventionalised, univocal language. In other words, abstraction as subsumption renders networks unidirectional, gears them to the intentionality of specific projects and so generates a hierarchy of social practices and subjectivities.

Operationalising Formal Structures: de Certeau and the Metaphorisation of Formal Codes

At the same time, the existence (being) of abstractions depends on an ability to operationalise them. Whilst the formal rationality of bureaucratic organisations issues in a system of rules, the rules themselves must be applied to concrete situations in order to sustain their legitimacy. This conversely requires the concretisation of the rule concept: to see how its actualisation can be achieved its conditions of possibility or grounds, its 'relevances' (Schutz, 1970, p.12) must be accessed.

It is important to see this as a discursive process as well as one which takes place in time and space. As de Certeau (1984, pp. 31–2) has argued, the operationalisation of social codes involves their metaphorisation. In this way, their content can be translated to new situations and fields of reference.

Crucially, this sense of their metonymic structure enables agents to appropriate codes, although in his example, colonial codes, this doesn't initiate a translation to a new field of reference, rather they remain 'other' and 'assimilated...externally' by the 'dominant order'. Presumably, this state of affairs was due in part to the absence of a paradigm contesting the political settlement of colonisation. However, accommodations within the paradigm parallel the case of bureaucracy where generally, translations do not issue in a paradigm shift.

Metaphorisation is transformative work which, as Waldron (1967, p.167) notes 'selects', 'suppresses', 'organises' the subject/concept's structure by applying to it features that normally apply to its predicate. In other words, it serves to shift the centre of gravity of the existing formal codes/structure. The colonised Amerindians are still operating the same code but with different inflections from the official reading.

This entails that these instances of operationalisation remain an enunciative gap or void in the dominant discourse; they are invisible except as the efficacy of formal institutional action which masks this work as the legitimacy of the dominant order.

As argued in Chapters 2 and 4, the application of abstractions in the here and now involves an act of synthesis between concept and situation. Further, this moment is suppressed in formal institutions where the abstractional process is such that the initial state of affairs or agency appears to 'magically' give rise to a product and the actual production itself is displaced. This lack of process or mediation means that the relationship between action and outcome appears arbitrary, purely instrumental, rather than a specific link or articulation; it remains a silence in discursive practice. de Certeau (op. cit., p.101) notes this point when he indicates the way codes, taken in the abstract, perform a 'literal' or 'faceless' role as placeholders of signification, in other words, their 'equivocalness' between significations. This equivocalness is characterised by de Certeau (op. cit., p.100) as a kind of arbitrariness, as being like the way a 'tremulous image confuses and multiplies' its object.

It has previously been suggested here that the relationship between formal institutional practices and lived reality ('living labour' for example) is dualistic, that one is ontologically external to the other (Chapter 3) but that a kind of coherence of signification is achieved as 'system' mimics 'lifeworld'. de Certeau's observations fit this model where abstractional placeholders mimic rather than articulate, or give expression to, the lived quality of the doxa of everyday life. As Arthur (op. cit., p. 41) has argued in the case of money as an 'empty universal', an equivalencer of concrete things, such placeholders are pure form, form without content, a kind of fetish object. Their presence in lived reality is simply a 'presence', an uncanny resemblance.

Equivocation or Vaciller: The Homo Clausus and Constitutive Gaps of the Social

As argued above, the workings of such equivocation within modern capitalism are the hallmark of real abstraction. Formal institutions with their Weberian impersonality equivalence concrete activities and individuals such that their mediational processes, as Halewood argues, are displaced, producing an actual fragmentation of social practices into discrete roles figuring abstract 'persons', the separation of agency from structure, and so on.

> The relations between persons…and things, or between things and things are not treated primarily as relations, or as in process but as things in themselves (op. cit., p.159)

Elias's response to the agency-structure problem implicated here describes the autonomous individual of this formulation of social relations as the *homo clausus*. However, as du Gay (2008) puts this in relation to Elias and later (ibid., pp. 48–9), to Weber's account of the rise of capitalism and its distinctive 'personalities' or roles:

> Elias is keen to indicate that he does not view the self-perception that find expression in the image of man (*sic*) as *homo clausus* as an outright illusion. It exists but does so in specific ways in relation to specific purposes and activities. (ibid., p.30)

This self-governing individual and their religio-capitalistic context evidenced *inter alia* a kind of personhood (the Methodist and so on), as argued in Chapter 2, which was characterised by Weber's 'salvation anxiety', a sense of incoherence about the self and its relation to the divinity such that the individual was perpetually poised in a *vaciller* between heaven and hell, and could not translate into the category of the 'saved'. This graphically captures the nature of modern capitalism in that although we can operationalise the system it always remains beyond or other in that our actions are subsumed as echoes of its own logic, that is, as equivalenced by it. This equivalencing is the silencing of the agent's own concrete narrative, a gap produced by abstractional subsumption which within that discourse is real, a void or enunciative gap at the same time constitutive of formal discourse.

The *homo clausus*, as we've suggested, is, as per Halewood, a representation of that gap. Sociological analysis by concentrating on entities rather than process has often failed to move beyond abstractional dualisms which echo the formal institutional framework of modern capitalism rather than interrogating it; agency v. structure, micro v. macro, discrete levels of social reality, and so on. This is why metaphorisation and translation are important ideas: they enable us to see how the 'gaps' or differences and entities entailed by sociological compartmentalisation are really moments of a process. As was indicated earlier in the discussion of Barthes' haiku it is only possible to see how entities are related and emerge from one another if we are prepared to think discursive practices differently. The haiku worked because it was possible to shift from thinking of the event it describes in terms of discrete states related causally to rather seeing an outcome or realisation (*seism*) as coincident with the process through which it is arrived at. In other words, there was a shift to thinking systemically about the relation between the terms, that is, to a synchronic rather than purely diachronic view. Here the translation is not the event itself but rather its coexistence with its outcome; it is on-going, inherent in and, other things being equal, continually reproducing the 'end state'. This is important because it shows that there is a 'reversible' quality about outcomes or entities; they can be viewed as always in dynamic tension with the context in which they arise and hence open to different possible trajectories, futures.

The discussion of Balzac's literary style was used to illustrate this point in Chapter 4 and more generally the lability within signifier/signified or subject/predicate relations; what is a thing at one point is a process at another, process itself becomes 'to process'. Translation represents this when what was the major topic becomes subsidiary, a way of talking about something else. du Gay's (1997, pp.13–17) oft-cited case of the Walkman as a 'translation' of walkie-talkie, cassette player, stereo system and so on, from one 'semantic network' to another serves as an instance here. As du Gay indicates, the process element is always there, sedimented in the outcome. This lends the latter and its translation a sense of hybridity, the artefact is 'reversible' or open to repurposing. This trope is evidenced in the re-emergence of 'retro' technologies such as the vinyl record or cassette player.

If, in contrast to this, the focus shifts to entities rather than the coproduction of entities by their circumstances of emergence then *inter alia* we arrive at the *homo clausus*. This is, as we argued, nonetheless real, although not in the 'universal' or species sense of the 'being human', as Elias notes (du Gay. 2008, p.30). Although he is not explicit about this du Gay's case study of the self-service shopper as a self-governing individual put together through training, a scripted space of equipment, rules and practices – a techno-social assemblage or agencement – demonstrates how such a personage or ideal type can be assembled. Foucault's (1999, pp.97–100) work on hierarchical observation likewise evinces the production of self-governing individuals as positionalities via disciplinary regimes and at a wider horizon of generality, discursive formations.

However, du Gay's focus on the mechanics of interpellation of the individual subject and its decentering within the assemblages of self-service shopping means that he ignores the wider questions of what constitutes the formal institutional context of shopping itself.

Light can perhaps be shed on this via a return to Hegel's (op. cit., pp.1945) observation on the state: this is a context within which things and services are equivalenced through money, 'an extreme culmination of externality', the 'really existent value of both things and services'. It is simply the radical externality of this formal equivalencing and, in effect, formal rationality to the concrete world that marks out modern capitalism and makes hierarchisation possible. In other words, it is the external arbitration of values and so statuses (through a fetish object or placeholder), their impersonal mediation, rather than their negotiation with living beings which involves an act of recognition of the particularities of groups and individuals that marks out the formal institutional positioning of subjects. Formal rationality is nonetheless contested collectively, and so the institutional complex of the capitalist state is willy nilly forced to engaged with this 'unreal' (lived) world but only on the basis of how the quantification of people and things should be done. On the other hand, institutional life picks up on the informally practiced values it is confronted with. Occupants of roles must display 'self-generated' qualities of integrity, a desire for co-operation, commitment, trust, ability to share and be transparent with colleagues and so on, although these terms function as placeholders whose content is infinitely labile. This social construction of the *homo clausus* is, as we've argued, an illustration of the process of real abstraction, living labour becomes abstract labour, consumption is scripted by corporations and so on. However in order to get a purchase these processes rely on something they hide, the common sense world of the subject's experiential life and its recuperation of the *homo clausus* as the doxa of autonomy. As Habermas (1999, pp. 174–5) has noted the types existing in the common sense of the lifeworld are invaded by system imperatives and these idealisations then appear in 'a typical fashion' as concrete and real idealisations.[76]

Usefully here Khatib's (2013, p.4) reflections on Benjamin's *Arcades Project* and his phantasmagoria of modern urban life cast light on the basis of the related idea of abstraction in material practices, the experience of embodiment of abstraction in everyday life how subjects and their environments are put together in commodified relations. Such

> phantasmagoria are not mere illusions but designate a certain type of phenomena, which have acquired a material density and stability in capitalist everyday life the bourgeois interior, urban places, sociological types and architecture... he states, 'With the Haussmannisation of Paris, the phantasmagoria was rendered in stone'.

Similarly, Wolfarth[77] (cited in Khatib, op. cit., p.4) observes that phantasmagoria are not merely items of 'false consciousness of ideological discourse' rather they are 'materialised in space, objects and practices'. It would follow from this that in some sense the types or personages of the religious spirit of capitalism or of the consumer really do exist. Weber's types represent 'real idealisations'. In some sense, these are then embodied forms of *homo clausus,* a point perhaps reinforced by Halewood's (op. cit., p.147) questioning of whether the gender types Man and Woman 'are only abstractions in thought'.

It has been argued that all these examples are suggestive of forms of subsumption and estrangement of the individual or social groups within a framework which is both juridical and in a more localised sense, institutional. At

---

[76] Although Habermas focuses here on the substitution of types for lived realities and a colonisation rather than the 'sensuous supersensuous' as such.

[77] Wolfarth, I. (1996), p.199.

the same time, it is a system of gaps, as is implied by Lukács' (1971) investigation of the interweaving of bureaucracy and commodification to which the focus now shifts.

Lukács and Fragmentation

While Lukács' (op. cit., p.92) account of the reification in commodity-based social formations seems correct in pinpointing the 'isolated commodity owner' as a product of 'rational and isolated acts of exchange', the discussion glosses over how individuals manage to coordinate their existences. Perhaps the difficulty lies in his characterising the reification as boundaries to the individual, as per Elias's *homo clausus*. By contrast, what is required for present purposes is a perceptual switch through which boundaries are seen as voids in the formal structures of capitalism, a suppressed content through which capitalism is actualised in the here and now and also through which opposition to its abstractional effects is organised.

The problem of organising the fragments of capitalism was recognised by the neo-liberal Hayek, who observed

> How can the combination of fragments of knowledge existing in different minds bring about the results which, if they were to be brought about deliberately, would require a knowledge on the part of the directing mind which no single person can possess. (Hayek cited in Metcalf, 2017, p.30)

and came to a different conclusion: the capitalist market had 'a kind of mind' (loc. cit.). Whilst recognising that capitalism has its own logic, that of formal equivalencing of concrete entities and values in different market situations, Hayek seems be saying not only that but also that it organises itself above and beyond its spatio-temporal conditions of existence, clearly another form of reification of exchange relations.[78] Contrary to Hayek, the success in the U.K. of 'the City', for example, is widely known to depend on its lifeworld of densely

---

[78] This is not the same as 'mind' normally understood. It seems closer to 'logic', that is, a closed analytic system, in contrast to mind as including a reflexive capacity. That is, the 'logic of capital' version of mind can't really be seen as something that can take the position of the other. As argued previously concrete labour is nothing to capital. Reflexivity is substituted by colonisation of labour power in this context.

structured informal gatherings in cafes, pubs and restaurants where information is exchanged. These gaps of suppressed sociality are in reality the sources of coordination, the intersubjective content through which the formal structures are mobilised.

The negotiation of complex coordinated action in the market can be accounted for along the lines indicated by Dummett's (1981, p.461) Context Principle of the indexicality of communicative practices where agents indicate to others not just their immediate moves but a whole practice, which is conveyed, referenced, analogically. Its indexical features, the shared symbolic resources of a practice, are not just unspoken here but suppressed by instrumentalisation, the abstraction of action from concrete context and its equation with an outcome in a 'closed system' of market predictions. As Hayek's 'transcendental' solution indicates, this shared area of practice is occulted and outcomes appear as if magicked into existence.

Lukács' account of these exchange relations brings together the formal rational features of bureaucracy as epitomised by the modern state with the rational calculative aspects of capitalism as a generalised system of production and accumulation. He follows Weber in viewing capitalism and the modern state as having 'structural similarity': He cites Weber:

Both are...quite similar in their fundamental nature...the modern capitalist concern is based inwardly above all on calculation. It requires a system of justice and an administration whose workings can be rationally calculated, at least in principle. It is as little able to tolerate the dispensing of justice according the judge's sense of fair play in individual cases or any other irrational means or principles...as it is able to endure [the 'caprice, or sense of mercy'] of a patriarchal administration...' (ibid., pp. 95–6).

Lukács notes this sense of abstract rationality displacing the individual case which serves to isolate the concrete person by commodity relations in his narrative. This then by default indicates gaps or voids, the 'isolated acts of exchange'. It similarly links the formal rationality of 'closed' specialised systems (ibid., p.89) and its displacement of concrete individuals such that individual deviations from an ideal scripting appear as 'mere sources of error', as a nothing, rather than different ways doing things. Further, he notes the loss of individual uniqueness to the trope of 'formal equality' (ibid., p.87) the space between role and personality disappears. It is worth noting that at the time of the early Lukács and even earlier that of Hegel, the effects of rationalisation on the personality of the individual were still a live topic whilst nowadays the elision of personality and role is registered largely in terms of an unarticulated unease which can be ameliorated by various 'therapies'.

The Voids of Social Ontology

Earlier Hegel (op. cit., pp.194–5) had seen this trait of abstract equivalencing in the emergence of the modern state and observed it as an 'extreme culmination of externality'. It wasn't just that the state was a structure which impacted on the individual as something with its own emergent properties but rather that the state was wholly separate, it functioned in a different ontological register from concrete living beings. An analogy for this extreme externality can perhaps be seen in the way oil droplets in the sea are shaped by the movement of the currents: the water shapes the oil droplet from the outside, the droplet mimics the movement of the currents without ever becoming a part or relation of what it echoes.

However, as Arthur (2001, *passim*) has argued in relation to capital, these two worlds, although 'nothing' to each other qua abstract and concrete labour are nevertheless inextricably intertwined, modern capitalism depends on this lived world of free/informal interrelation which it in turn attempts to systematise or colonise to use Habermas's (1999) diction. Conversely, this abstraction is an illusion, a nothing, seen from the point of view of everyday life, where it is seen as unnecessary to achieve results and where social relations take a different form, where we exist, according to Merleau-Ponty (1992a, p.10), as *semblables*, equal but plural networks of neighbours,[79] whilst it is also real from the point of view of capital's self-actualising accumulation.

Ontological priority

This discussion has taken the lived world of the everyday as foundational and so ontological priority is seen as going to concrete labour and interrelation in these schemes and hence the non-hierarchised or *semblablesque* mode of

---

[79] These could be 'micro' or 'macro': a conversation, or a social group, voluntary organisation, movement, an event, for example.

relation is seen as the ground for hierarchy and generally, the subsumption of individuals within modern capitalism.

It is worth noting that the term 'structure'generally connotes formal institutional relations and interrelations (state and class, work, education links and so on) although this is often not spelled out. Hence here structures are seen as grounded in exchange relations; the exchange of services or things for money, that is, they are seen as property relations. It is consequently not surprising that in much social theorising an abstract dualism displaces discussion of 'structure' in the more concrete or *sembablesque* sense of collectivities and the informal distribution of power within them, as per Miliband's (1970) interlocking networks of power, the informal interrelations between the state and its ruling class.

The theme of abstract dualism brings us back to Giddens: despite an absence of the formal/informal distinction regarding structure Giddens' critique of dualism is perceptive in seeing processes qua social practices as key to understanding the entities agency and structure. Further, it would be wrong to see Giddens as necessarily equivalencing agency and structure in an 'extreme' identitarian way (Parker, 2000, p.77) through practices. The articulation of practices in specific contexts can produce different kinds of outcomes regarding the 'duality'. For example, practices within voluntary organisations, pub quiz teams or social movements can give more scope to forms of agency than practices in an army, factory or office. It follows that the content of 'social practice' is not to be sought within the practice in isolation but rather in the way it is articulated in concrete situations. Practice as process is not a discrete entity external to socially objectified states but rather should be seen as a moment of those states and vice versa. As mentioned above, the tradition of social theorising is weighted (positivistically) towards difference (compartments, levels, discrete entities) between things or states rather than their connections, resemblances whereas it is argued here that 'difference' should be seen as mediated by resemblance; the priority should go to connection and synthesis. Without this ground, accounts of emergent structures or terms lack coherence of reference; they do not relate to or reference their conditions of emergence, they lack a reflexive awareness.

Whilst emphasising this practice or process aspect of enquiry Giddens' approach fails to deal with hierarchical subsumption, the way the state imposes a politico-juridical form on Elias's (op. cit., p.261) 'networks of interdependencies... a structure of mutually oriented and dependent people'. On the more localised terrain he ignores, for example, Foucault's (1999) 'hierarchical observation' or the structuring of roles within formal organisations which arguably articulates and coproduces the state's power and distributes it through discursive formations.

So Giddens and Mouzelis are both partially right in their separate ways. Giddens' neglect of the ontological gap between formal and informal life is offset by a focus on the processual spatial-temporal continuities of social practices and agents' ability to operate across this divide. Hence arguably, the way in which Giddens is wrong is more productive than Mouzelis's manner of being right and in what follows Giddens can be read in this way, that is, against himself, as providing an account of networks which form the material of subsumption within formal organisations.

Giddens, Time-Space Distantiation and Its Significance for Simultaneity/Co-ordination

In his discussion of time-space distantiation, Giddens (op. cit., p.304) argues for an idea of 'structures [which] refer to a virtual order of relations', an absent presence in any interaction involving co-presence. Such interaction 'is structurally implicated in systems of broad time-space distantiation...how such systems span large sectors of time-space. (ibid., xxvi). In order to understand the relationship between agency and structure, '...we have to see how the practices...are embedded in wider reaches of time and space...to discover their relation to institutionalised practices' (ibid., p.298).

This suggests, although Giddens never spells out this implication, the coordination or simultaneity of past and present temporalities: rhythms, routines, practices. This entailment is seen in his discussion of Willis's *Learning to Labour*. Here not only are different contemporaneous contexts or social worlds co-ordinated and reproduced, but moreover, past experiences weigh on the present, the transmission of parent culture, 'life on the shop floor', 'working class communities', the 'neighbourhood and the street' (ibid., p.299). Hence we have a cross-section of different past temporal structures or temporalities as well as coordination across different contemporaneous spaces. The effect is to flatten past and present out and to suggest a moment of social process in which past and present have a simultaneity through which they are co-ordinated.

Willis's study suggests that the academic failures/resisters to academic success have access to the experience of other generations, for example, the parent culture and that this coordination is implicit in his notion of social reproduction where the past as routinised praxis reproduces itself in the situated present and so must be present to us in the here and now in some sense.

Again, Giddens' (op. cit., pp.77–8) use of Sartre's example of the seriality of the bus queue 'demonstrates the mutual coupling of time-space relations of presence and absence' which is 'channelled' through regularised contexts or 'locales' where presencing occurs via bracketing the distantiated locales. Here the bus queue is an intersection of different constituencies of the traveller; residence, work, public transport, local government politics and so on. In this way, it represents a punctualisation of relations in 'broad time-space distantiation'.

Co-ordination and its intellectual background

This sense of co-ordination across time and space is voiced in the early Feuerbach's view that simultaneity is as important as historical progression (*Aufhebung*) and as seen here is echoed, in Giddens' view that other situations are present to us when we act and that we act through them. Feuerbach (1987, pp.95–6) suggests that in some sense time and its spaces unfold to provide a spatialised moment of history, a moment in which space subverts time as totalised presentness. For him, the traditional Hegelian view 'knows only subordination and succession; co-ordination and succession are unknown to it'. By contrast, for Feuerbach, succeeding stages in history also form 'moments in a simultaneous totality' which means that subsumption and coordination co-determine each other instead of the linearity entailed by *Aufhebung* taken on its own. Coordination therefore contains subsumption and vice versa, so crucially for this argument coordination overdetermines subsumption, thus producing a conflictual mode of interrelation, reciprocity. This aspect of coordination will be pursued later via Beauvoir's development of the idea.

It can be argued that Feuerbach's notion of coordination also entails a sense that everything appears as connected through any given situation and structured by that situation, according to its own movement, trajectory, horizon, and thus represents an idea of network, a way in which everything is connected according to a present locale, rather than preordained in an historicist way This inevitably raises the question of how we are to think historical change as a subsumption of past times and places in a way that is consonant with the idea of their synchronicity/coordination developed above. Barbaras (op. cit., pp145–6) argues that historical

> movement requires a radicalisation of the Aristotelian concept…that requires that we abandon the notion of an immutable foundation in order to conceive of it as what creates its own unity rather than receiving it from this foundation.

In this view, as addressed in various ways above, beginning states, processes and outcomes codetermine each other. This sense of the interruption of the past by the present is also found in Benjamin's account of historical interpretation, as Khatib (2016, pp.202–3) has noted. Benjamin offers a notion of

> how to conceive a historical mode of presentation avoiding both the flat historicisation and hermetic dehistoricisation. If according to Benjamin 'what is at stake is not to present literary works in the context of their age, but to present the age that perceives them, our age, in the age during which they arose'. The task is to construct the text through its gaps and read them not as gaps but as symptomatic lacunae.

Perhaps in this way we can see our times as the other of past temporalisations which then reflexively suggest the gaps or suppressions as interruptions of the historical present. As Khatib (loc. cit.) has it: '…what is the non-contemporaneous signature of the self-eternalising time of capitalism…?' Or, perhaps, another way of putting this would be 'What is the everyday of capitalism and do Barbaras and Benjamin provide an aid to grasping its continuities over different times and places?'

All of this suggests a way or moment in which the present recuperates the past rather than is dominated by it as social commentators such as Bourdieu (2006, p.79) tend to suggest ('It's yesterday's man who inevitably predominates in us', Durkheim cited approvingly in *Outline*). This is not to argue of course that history does not co-determine the construction of situation.[80]

The importance of Feuerbach's revision of Hegel's dialectic is that it enables us to see how objectifications can be challenged, transgressed by a content which both connects with but also exposes the limits of objectification, the point where meaning becomes diffuse. More precisely, coordination disrupts *Aufhebung*, renders succession, hierarchisation visible as a process, we can see how networks get co-opted. Thus it is possible to draw on otherwise opaque socio-historical resources in the way that Giddens' time-space distantiation suggests; we can join up the dots in what Foucault (1982, p.119) styles the 'fragmented form of the enunciative field' of organisations.

There are various expressions of this kind of coordination and the way it opens up forms of subsumption, whether we couch these in sociological, literary, historical etc. terms. The discussion above deals with historical subsumption and there are similarities between Feuerbach's idea of the subversion of *Aufhebung* and Adorno's (1973, pp. 163, 183) notion that the concept is always accompanied by what it subsumes as its non-identical, displaced identity. Merleau-Ponty's (1992b, pp.94–5) 'hyperdialectic', as above, also shows the co-existence of historical subsumption and its co-determination by the historical present or 'situation'[80]. In terms of the literary, Wood's (2008, pp.13–14) discussion of Balzac exemplifies the idea that there is a tension in language between conventionalised and metaphorical tropes, forms of understanding; one where free association communicates the sense of context and another where the reader is instructed or led in a 'readerly' way through a text, subsuming their intentions within its preordained plan. In all of these cases, there is an implication that hierarchisation can be opened up to what in reality is its ground, that abstraction, hierarchy etc. is always somehow both dependent on the simultaneity of coordinated linkages pointed up by Feuerbach and potentially subverted by it, depending on the politics of situation.

Subsumption and the everyday: Lefebvre, cycles v. linear 'modernisation'

To develop this point: one way of thinking about subsumption is as Lefebvre suggests, the way the everyday, routine, 'cyclic' temporalities which structure the customary fabric of life are thrown into juxtaposition with the temporalities of modernisation, whether of capital or the state. Lefebvre (2002, pp.60–61) argues that the 'cohesion' of society is threatened by the heterogeneity of the everyday and its collision with the 'linear' pattern of the accumulation process. Capitalism attempts to control the changes that take place in everyday life, the cycles of fashion, taste and so on, but can only accelerate these and mask them

---

[80] The 'global-local nexus' fits this socio-historical model as the subsuming abstraction 'global' is co-dependent on its correlate 'local', the concrete, particular context.

with its linearity, presenting the past of urban life for example, as an unbroken continuum rather than the episodic reality of urbanism. The very fissiporousness of the everyday is manifest in the mutations of alternative or oppositional forms of culture, the 'creative underground' where art, fashion, music are forever undergoing mutation according to dynamics of locale.[81]

It is the clash between these two forms of temporalisation that provides the opening, the reflexive grasp of social process, the notion that modern capitalism has its own ineluctable logic and trajectory which threatens existing forms of the everyday. Urban redevelopment is one obvious example where the black boxes, to use Latour's (1987) parlance for the taken for granted, get opened and people can see the real constraints, forms of oppression that they are up against.

Whilst Giddens' account of routinisation and temporal rhythms acknowledges the heterogeneity of 'daily life' there is no sense that there are unresolvable disorienting displacements of the radical kind that Lefebvre identifies between the everyday and 'linear accumulation' as we've further argued exist where individuals or collectivities are equivalenced via abstract formulae, the rational calculative. The identification of networks as a way of avoiding abstractional displacements and as accomplishing the bracketing/ presencing of events in time-space locales is seen as a way forward here.

In what follows, it is argued that networks facilitate closure differently, that is, via the kind of heterogeneity intrinsic to the everyday. Networks, like the open or writerly text, follow the logic of metaphorisation and thus facilitate switches in perspective and configuration as per Wood's Balzac illustration. Networks therefore engender enclosure and disclosure: they promote the articulation of the doxa which makes visible the invisible processes of coordination whilst at the same time bracketing other linkages as the doxa (everyday) of the new focus and social relations are hence discursively reconfigured.

A distinction should be made here between the routine doxic element of the everyday (everydayness) and those moments where it disrupts and fissiparates linear processes of subsumption.[82] It is also worth noting that the routinisation of meaning, the conventionalisation (*usure*) of metaphor/discursive practice, as seen in Chapter 4, where agents become 'stuck', dominated by established codes – meaning works behind our backs – would still be an issue even where

---

[81] See for example Clements (2017) on the rich diversity of 'underground' culture and its strategies of recuperation in a context of commodification.

[82] See comment on Lefebvre in Osborne (1995), p.194.

abstractional subsumption doesn't occur, that is, in the context of colleagial interdependency. Here concrete problems are likely to be seen as situational, more particular or personalised rather than being displaced by role or market forces. We now turn to look at an example of networks without subsumption.

The Linux Open Source Network

The following is an illustration of how this conflict between subsuming organisational power and the popular, every day, informal network becomes visible. Linux Open Source computer programming (Kelion, 2012) offers a way of linking various trade products such as Microsoft's Windows packages to free software which in important ways parallels and provides access to those packages, i.e. provides alternative access to computing and the Internet. Microsoft (loc.cit.) described Open Source programmes as 'a cancer' and 'un-American'. The case of Linux reveals both the possibility that using the Internet can be improvised and controlled by users and renders visible the subsumption of networking by powerful organisations; one can see how Microsoft is ultimately dependent on coordination because Open Source does what they do without formal hierarchy. The politics of the Internet is revealed, shown to function through the occlusivity of subsumption, that is networking is made mysterious rather than every day; it is blackboxed.

Weber (2005, p.262) notes the mutual exclusiveness of hierarchies and networks in the world of software production: absence of bureaucratic authority and market structures from networks means that the de facto division of labour between the network and the hierarchy (even in a conflictual relationship) needs a coordination mechanism, but neither price nor authority will cross the interface successfully and that there is a distinctive 'ontology of hierarchical actors' (ibid., p.302, n.80).

He further observes that innovation happens at the intersection of hierarchy and network (where, for instance, network teams come up with a solution to a problem that Microsoft et al. haven't fixed) as with Lefebvre's notion of cycles of activity interrupting 'linear accumulation', something that disrupts the everyday of user-producer relations. This occurs, for example, through the compatibility of Linux and Microsoft software packages; this is an innovative synthesis, a reverse appropriation by volunteers and enthusiasts in open source, the informal integration of artefacts from the commodity form. However, as he also notes, innovation happens within network structures themselves, that is, the routinisation of problem solving is disrupted by 'forking' or moving onto a new project. More commonly, innovation happens at the periphery and thus can shift the power balance within the network

> The decision about when and how to innovate lies with the user on the edge of the network [via 'non-discriminatory' access to elements of operating system/source code-H.F.]. The centre does not really control the process as much as incorporate pieces of innovation into itself. And if it fails to do so successfully, a new centre can always form at what was formerly an edge (ibid., p. 233).

This also is an instance of the disruption of routinisation. Arguably, it resembles Barthes' haiku illustration in that the conventionalisation of internet source coding procedures leads to a confrontation with a problem presented by the ordinary, everyday contingency of the situation that can't be contained without transformation of the field of reference. This is a moment of seism or reflexivity ('commentary') in which the agent stands outside themselves, as identified by the problem, as repositioned by it. Hence the dead conventionalised discourse is re-enlivened.[83] de Certeau's insights on the re-enlivening or metaphorisation of codes and conventions could also signal an appropriation within an existing field or paradigm as occurred in the Amerindian syncretisation of the cultural codes of Spanish colonisers (see Chapter 4).

As Weber observes, the innovative productivity of the network structure has been widely noted and large organisations have attempted to adopt forms of it where they are closely interconnected. This however occurs within an intellectual context in which theorists' ideas

---

[83] Unlike Derrida's (1974, p.11) account of usure, here it is not of itself considered to lead to abstractional polarisations or aporias – e.g. nature v. culture – as abstract conventionalised language can still, following Dummett's (1981, p. 83 ff) notion of indexicality, refer or articulate via the context of utterance. Meaning is thus considered not to reside in language itself but in the performative context. In this instance, translation works purely analogically, 'It's like X…'.

...still suffer from an unfortunate 'bracketing' of the hierarchical structures [taking them as the ground of networks – H.F.] as that which is somehow 'real' or concrete, while trying to prove that networks 'matter' vis a vis more traditional structures (ibid., p. 263).

Hence in this scenario the hierarchy does no more than mimic the network which in turn serves to mask its supervening power. Weber (op. cit., p.302, n.80) goes on to suggest that recognising the hiatus between hierarchies and networks could provide 'a more differentiated view of the nature of an evolving political space' which could be taken as 'global civil society'. This might be one way of taking forward Lefebvre's idea of the recuperation of human relations in the everyday.

In sum, we've noted the homology between the network structure and metaphorisation, the processual element of the innovative, translations and otherwise metaphoric (de Certeau) transformations of codes and conventions. The network itself serves as a medium, the everyday of the transformation; it constitutes an intersubjective moment in which the routine ('unconscious') coordination of the collectivity takes place.

Hence networks, as opposed to hierarchies present a context, an open discursive structure, in which an articulation or translation of the everyday can be made. As they constitute peer-to–peer interrelations, they resonate with the doxa of colleagiality (team spirit, neighbourliness, friendship, co-operation, 'we're all pulling/in this together', and so on). Through routinisation/*usure* networks work behind our backs but this doxa is translatable, can be made visible, and recuperable, unlike with the abstractional forms of equivalencing seen in bureaucratic authority and the market whose logic follows trajectories which are external to lived reality.

Teams and Co-Ordination: Another Way of Thinking About Informal Agency Within Hierarchised Structures

Organisations frequently use 'team' or network strategies as these are believed to increase potential for innovation, synergies, information flow, cross fertilisation and so on, via in effect creating new discursive formations. It's an attempt to objectify, render visible, processes that go on anyway as the organisation's taken for granted or black-boxed modus operandi. Hence formal 'teamwork' etc. is the misrecognition of the way the organisation actually functions, that is, the coordination, networks, interrelations which have been already subsumed as the ground of its bureaucratised structures. Company human relations techniques therefore attempt to harness the drift of such informal logics for the benefit of their telos. However, this is a case of the uncanny (already seen), as organisational strategy takes management ideas as its apparent ground (as above on preordinance of hierarchy) by reproducing in objectified form something that already goes on informally.

Informal networks themselves produce subjects (Bourdieu's subjects of coordination of action, for instance) and their subjectivity reflects the trope of interrelation in that subjects relate reflexively to themselves as the networked other. In this mode, they have access to what, under hierarchical subsumption would pass as blackboxed, *epoché,* invisible. Networks entail synchronicity and synthesis, rather than the analytic of temporal succession and subsumption experienced in bureaucratic relationships. We can see this as pre-eminently expressed in the idea of synergy where interrelation as coordination is seen in Sartre's (1982, pp.379–82) 'regulatory third', for example. In this case, totalised praxis itself constitutes a kind of network structure against which action is measured. As such, networks have an extraordinary potential to mediate/coordinate the actions of those who create them. It is argued here that subjects' trajectories are bound up in 'simultaneous totalities' which represent something new and generally unpredictable as they rely on the bracketed circuitry in which those agents move to create something beyond the logo-centric via negotiation or contestation of the latter[84].

We can see then that subjects relate to another in the mediated way that the other is given to the subject, that is, as the subject's otherness. In coordination of activities with other subjects, it is therefore its own sense of relation that the subject has to negotiate, rather than a direct relation to another as directly given to the subject's consciousness. Elsewhere Mead (1970, pp.152–64) expresses a cognate idea: relating via the 'generalised other', and so on. This is a 'different', non-identical subject which exists in relation to, mediates self-identity. In other words, the other is given via its relationality, as for example, Sartre's regulatory third (mediational other) shows.

Harvey's concept of relational space is also productive here in that it enables us to view the subject as a coordinated existent constituted across different physical spaces. The abstractions of the value form 'internalise the whole

---

[84] See, for instance, Strauss (1964) above on negotiation.

historical geography of innumerable labour processes in the space-time of the world market' (Harvey, 2006, p.289) and for this relational space 'there is an important sense in which a point in space 'contains' all other points' if we look at retail or demography, for example (Harvey, cited in Sheppard, 2006, p.124). Capital as the subject's abstractional other works regardless of conscious grasp of the value form in its coordination.

Capital's bureaucratised organisational structures serve to damp down the synthesising moment of coordination by preventing its emergence as the visible.[85]Totality, becomes marginalised, residual to capital, inaccessible to social experience, it becomes everyday as Lefebvre (op. cit., p.32) argues in the sense that it is fragmented, co-opted and thus 'masked' by capitalist modernity (ibid., p.24). Hence networking as everyday coordination is subsumed within a bureaucratic carapace which lives off it. 'Team', 'interaction', 'dialogue' etc. serve as placeholders or covers for rational-legal abstraction and commodification. Commodified relations appear in the guise of everyday, free interaction (ibid., pp.24–5). However, it's important to grasp that abstraction/subsumption depends on relational factors of a different, non-chronic sort, those of simultaneity of concrete existence, or as Harvey (2010, pp. 134–5) puts it, the linking of different concrete spaces, activities. Even where variables ('activity spheres') are of differing significance,

...the dialectical tension within their uneven development should always be borne in mind...

Marx's whole account of the rise of capitalism out of feudalism can in fact be reconstructed and read in terms of a co-evolutionary movement between and across...different activity spheres...

The variables in this case are at one and the same time hierarchised, as weighted differently in 'uneven development', and co-evolutionary, that is reciprocally dependent whilst evolving differentially through time. In this way, the different temporal structures of capital and its concrete constituents become evident, those of succession and coordination. Process and outcome coproduce each other.

---

[85] Bureaucratic secrecy, instrumentalism and fetishistic perception illustrate the obstacles to visualisation posed by subsumption in the capitalist organisational complex.

We turn now to a closer examination of coordination in order to investigate in more detail what kind of ontological issues are at stake.

The Ontology of Co-ordination: Schutz, Goffman and Beauvoir

Schutz (1967, p.32) points out that people can carry out complex tasks involving the negotiation of formal rules, interpreting and applying them in specific contexts without much conscious effort. It is as if we are 'wired' to do this. Whether concerning working in shops, offices or playing chess we can respond quickly and/or effectively to tasks of the utmost complexity. It is as if people have a team as well as individual identity which allows them to co-ordinate their activities by reflex[86] rather than conscious deliberation. In other words, it can be argued that individuals in formal hierarchies also exist simultaneously as the ontological entity 'group' or 'team', individuals as *semblables* (Merleau-Ponty). Team behaviour is discussed in Goffman's *Presentation of Self in Everyday Life* where Goffman (p.85) observes that the 'emergent team impression…can conveniently be treated as a fact in its own right'.

In other words, the team behaviour of individuals, as Goffman (op. cit., pp.85–6) suggests, indicates that they do exist simultaneously in two different modes, as a discrete deliberative entity and also as a being interrelated, in coordination with/by others, a kind of composite existence. Goffman characterises the team as being different from any objectively instantiated group

…the individuals who are on the staff of an establishment are not members of a team by virtue of staff status but only by virtue of the cooperation which they maintain in order to sustain a given definition of the situation. Teams may be created by individuals to aid the group they are members of but they are acting as a team, not a group. Thus a team is a kind of secret society whose members may be known by non-members to constitute a society but the society these individuals are known to constitute is not the one they constitute by virtue of acting as members of a team (ibid., p.108).

---

[86] See also Connell, Wacquant and Young on body-reflexive practices, as cited in Woodward (2008), pp.97–104 and Redman (2008), pp. 177–8.

Therefore the 'society' stands as an objectified form or product of members' cooperation whilst the 'team' appears to be an intersubjective structure, performative and processual, rather than the effect or outcome of teamwork. We could, arguably, see objectification of the team as a group occurring via a switch in perception where one takes the position of the other, thus revealing through translation and identification of the operative field of reference the intersubjective processual content.

As Schutz (op. cit.) also argues, it is in this intersubjective mode that organisations function on an everyday basis. Coordination is routinely accomplished. As such here individuals do not use objectified ('rationalised') systems of rules of action.

We perform in factories and laboratories and offices highly 'rationalised' activities, we play chess together. How is this possible? (ibid., p.32)

It would involve

Frequently stringing together means and ends without clear knowledge 'about' their real connections (ibid., p.21)

This for Schutz represents an open horizonal structure of coordination entailing spontaneously reflexive 'deconstruction' of instrumentalist means – ends dualities associated with the rationalities of formal institutional life. It would thus represent the processual aspects implicit in outcomes, the suppressed multiple ways in which actual, lived relations are configured.

In order to make sense of how agents operate within coordination, Merleau-Ponty's (1994, p.94) idea of the intersubjective nature of relational process can be drawn on to fill out the picture in terms of the spontaneously reflexive nature of praxis as an objective moment which impinges on the subject from the outside, so to speak. It is

As if my mind emigrated into the scene it was in the process of setting for itself. I am snapped up by a second myself outside me; I perceive another.

Rather than implying an objectification *tout court* of the other it suggests that the self as part of the totality of praxis exists in an open relation with the discrete self, conditioning it or situating it and only thereby allowing its translation or realisation within a different social world. The other here can be taken to stand for the organisation over and against which the individual is figured; the way we are coordinated by our relationships in the process of coordinating them.

We can think of our interrelationships within the organisation as existing spatially, sharing a common space as *semblables* as well as existing as a structure of subsumption, that is, as hierarchy. Here subsumption is bracketed and operates through coordination. Hence whilst the team, say, as subsumed, takes commands from its leaders, its mode of praxis demands simultaneity rather than the chronic passage of discrete commands down a chain of positions. Each individual carries the other (team) with them and improvises conduct within the framework given by the other. The differentiations of role, position, status etc. are opened up here as a common spatial interrelation, each senses their dependency on the other and praxis/strategies entailed by this. Therefore, as per Goffman such networks include managers and to grasp the moment of coordination requires a kind of phenomenological reversal of hierarchy: it is as if hierarchy has been rotated sideways and the vertical becomes the horizontal. It is a perceptual translation from negotiation of formal statuses to the grasp of how these figure concretely as interrelations of individuals and groups; a shift in focus from the 'repair' of formal structures to the object domain or social worlds of teamwork and coordination which enable the 'repairs'.

Such a *Gestalt* transformation of hierarchy[87] reveals the horizontal links- trade union negotiation (collective and individual case work), working parties, team meetings, interdepartmental and interorganisational liaison, feedback exercises, and so on. This evidences a network structure more congruent with the unsuppressed articulation of intersubjective coordination outlined above in that it allows for some expression, on the margins, of a collaborative spirit.

As Weber's (2005) study shows, networks have a centre and a periphery but unlike formal hierarchies they have a dynamic and open ('metaphoric') structure such that the centre can translate or shift, realising a different social world. Doubtless, in the illustration of networks above, the centre would probably coalesce around figures or groups that are already central to the formal structure. The presence of other forms of interrelation does however emphasise the point

---

[87] Within the Gestalt image everything exists on one plane; there is an indifference to classification and hierarchy as a configuration of interconnections. The mind map represents one way of capturing this perceptual moment.

made throughout that organisations need this lateral unofficial form of relation in order to operationalise the formal structure.

Reciprocity, coordination and synchronicity

As the above discussion indicates, non-differentiated interrelatedness allows the individual to act in Bourdieu's (op. cit., p.80) insight both to coordinate and be coordinated, that is, the action of coordination coincides with and evokes, given the right praxis or habitus, coordination of action, interpellation of the subject. Habitus here involves the 'mastery of a common code' (ibid., p.81)[88]. In other words, action is simultaneously coordinated by what it coordinates. The social worlds, rhythms of practice of the participants hence intersect under these conditions as one space of coordination in 'teamwork'.

This returns us to Feuerbach's (op. cit., pp.95–6) critical comment that Hegel's emphasis on *Aufhebung* or subsumption disregards simultaneity, for the inference from teamwork is that although individuals experience their existence in diachronic mode as subsumption, they also have a different mode of being and experience where synchronicity or coordination is key and their existences may be seen as networked; where the differentiation associated with subordination is replaced by the differentiation of spatial location and intersection of social worlds, a co-evolutionary moment. One recalls here Beauvoir's (1972, p.17) argument that although men dominate women, they still require recognition in eyes of women, experience dependency on them and thus there is the basis for mutual relation. The argument here is moreover posed in more general terms:

...if following Hegel, we find in consciousness itself a fundamental hostility towards every other consciousness; the subject can be posed only in being

---

[88] This state-sponsored regulatory code is manifested in the illusion of a common language. However, there the argument seems to terminate. To be efficacious the language would have to be articulated with or by socio-linguistic groups, thus producing state coordination and geographical identity of language users but this would require it to be more than an illusion or idealisation. To be efficacious an entity must in some sense be real, in this case as an expression of state interpellation of its subjects, and possibly a candidate for real abstraction, something grasped by each group as particular and yet universal. In this case, illusion or misrecognition of the code (see Bourdieu, 2006, pp. 5, 43–4, 151–3) would not apply absolutely as in a sense the code is both. The error lies in eliding the ontological terrains of living language and the 'idealised' form (p.5).

opposed, he sets himself up as the essential, as opposed to the other, the inessential, the object.

But the other consciousness, the other ego, sets up a reciprocal claim... willy-nilly, individuals and groups are forced to recognise the reciprocity of their relations.

Each party is struggling for autonomy, which involves both fixing the other[89] as a condition of that and grasping that my freedom depends on recognition of that of the other and hence on solidarity. Previously Beauvoir had thus argued

I must grasp myself at the same time as object and freedom; I must recognise my situation as founded by the other, even while affirming my being beyond the situation [freedom] (Beauvoir, 1944, pp. 83–4) ...only the freedom of the other is able to give necessity to my being (ibid., pp. 95–6).[90]

Again, in Beauvoir's (1988, pp.161–2) conversations with Sartre the point is made that we exist in these two fundamental interrelated moments of connection and difference. I am one amongst others ('being on an equal footing, being just anyone at all') whilst at the same time having different qualities and in those respects I am unique from, and in that sense, superior to others, whether one is a writer or selling hot chestnuts ('the next man has his superiority').

From reciprocity to subsumption

The idea of reciprocity or interdependence can be elaborated in terms of how we have a sense of the other and their needs. This is clearly important in organisations. Goffman's 'teamwork' and Schutz's 'we-consciousness' are examples of this but how can we concretise this? Workers put into action the policy, plans and strategies of management, so in a sense they possess a kind of 'knowing as doing', they have a grasp of the intentionality or drift of management thinking/praxis by their being in the mode of relational other

---

[89] Earlier in the text the institutional basis of the male gaze was seen by Sandford as a major factor in what has been argued in this text to be subordination as a form of abstraction in contexts where men embody and mediate institutional and commodified positioning. Beauvoir's own view that individuals embody social relations is noted in the following section.

[90] Cited in Kruks (1990), pp. 86, 87.

discussed above. They can see how organisational decisions impact on them in the way their own behaviour is regulated, that is, its 'other' quality. This regulation by the other has a fluidity which falls between organisational and individual realities – it is contested and negotiated in an on-going way.

Further, from the other side, managers are engaged in the ongoing relational flow of negotiation, that is, with the being of the workforce. Therefore the subordination of the workforce is accompanied by a kind of reflexive give and take, a recognition that collaboration is experienced within capitalism as its unspoken fundamental nature, its raison d'etre. Hence there are two contradictory tendencies; one to subsume, control, define and the other to achieve reciprocation in the jointness of effort in the organisational context. This dialectic of collaboration and conflict, as the fundamental structure of interrelation, is experienced within capitalism as an absolute division between collaboration and control which reflects the fragmentation of functions and thus conflicts with the lived version of interrelation as negotiation. In extrapolating from Beauvoir, modern capitalism can be seen to co-opt the conflictual ego by suggesting its absolute autonomy as *homo clausus* with its narcissistic-seductive implications in the subject's desire for completion, and so the ghostly abstractional subject gains a purchase on the fundamental structure of interrelation.

This impacts on the lived sense of collaboration which is vitiated for the workforce by a sense of its provisional and attenuated nature as it is always mediated by the opacity of a subsumption seen as external and absolute and so is more than a conflictual mode of interrelation between confreres; it is one in which workers are not personally recognised, only appearing as roles, personifications of capital or institution.

In a reversal of hypostatised commodity relations, when negotiation is the topic, it has hierarchy as its bracketed or background content whilst in the case of non-recognition in occlusive abstractional subsumption, negotiation passes into the outcomes of capital-labour relations and the processual or intersubjective is lost and the outcome appears in fetish form without its concrete mediations, as if divorced from these. The displacement of the process of operationalisation then manifests itself in the guise of something quite external, 'management', a cover for the teamwork which goes on invisibly day-to-day.

On the other hand, as noted above, subsumed within the capital-labour relation is also a moment of reciprocity where the concrete worker engages with

155

the lifeworld of the manager; it is collegial in that workers tend to see managers as would-be workers that is, as potentially part of a team, people, they have to work *with*. From this perspective, the managerial view that managers represent the essence of the organisation seems unreal, an absurdity, a mystification or bureaucratic fragmentation of their actual roles as facilitators or technical experts. Hence workers share a kind of everyday critique of hierarchy/ subsumption in terms of concrete performance, 'X is useless' etc. This informal assessment of the manager as a team member highlights the character of intersubjective relations identified by Beauvoir above, they are both team, and individuated according to their specific qualities; they are reliant on the recognition from the other as one amongst others and also for their particular attributes as this duality of interrelation applies vis a vis the 'shopfloor'.

In sum, conclusions can be made as follows. Institutionally, the manager occupies the position of the regulatory other, but intersubjectively, this is also a position occupied by the team containing the manager, the regulatory third, in Sartre's terms, which represents the conditions of possibility of management. Hence as concrete lived relations this latter encapsulates the performance of self-management (*Autogestion*), where, in capitalism, institutional/bureaucratic subsumption appears as the non-being of the latter, its self-estrangement. Management is regulated here by what it regulates. All this of course remains suppressed, unarticulated in the institutional setting where it constitutes the self-other relation as self-relation.

Viewed from the classic paradigm of domination, Hegel's (1966) relation of lordship and bondsman, the bondsman's mediation of the script of rule is the flipside of domination where the lord's grasp of nature through the labour of the bondsman, a recognition of the other, is generalised but then fed back, as a directive translated in the actions of the bondsman.

Whilst this dialectic takes place in the relation of two consciousnesses, Beauvoir's conception of reciprocity presents an alternative to theories based on consciousness in the sense that it departs from a Hegelian idea of self-recognition and grounds itself on commonality of situation/being or embodiment rather than consciousness:

...if the body is not a *thing*, it is a situation as viewed in the perspective I am adopting – that of Heidegger, Sartre and Merleau-Ponty: it is the instrument of our grasp upon the world...(Beauvoir, 1972, p. 66).

Situation is therefore seen in terms of embodied being, that is, it embodies the individuals within it and so does not rely on conscious recognition but rather it is via shared experience of embodiment that situation generates reciprocity. The significance of this account of intersubjectivity is that teamwork and management can be seen as communicated situationally, knowledge is joint and performative and so questions of whether X interacts with Y as an individual rather than as embodied as situation or whether X grasps the utterances of Y propositionally are otiose.

The suppression of intersubjective narrative is noted in the work of Negt and Kluge (2015) who argue that the proletarian experience of life narrative as a continuum is rendered inaccessible via the institutional frameworks of modern capitalism. This echoes Lefebvre's account of the temporal structures of the latter and its suturing of the historical past. The discussion now moves to look at class as a central feature of this historical-developmental amnesia.[91]

---

[91] Negt and Kluge (2016, p.31ff) argue that the historical memory, self-understanding or intersubjectivity of the proletariat is suppressed but then recuperated as a fragmented form of its collective fantasy. An illustration that fits this is found in Horwell's (2020, p.6) description of the fantasy expressed in the work of fashion designer Kansai Yamamoto. His work was 'not subtle, tasteful, but the Japan of souvenir shops outside popular shrines stocked with tat in synthetic lamé; of firemen's demon tatoos; of woodblock prints of purple-clad ghosts. Yamamoto learned in time that these continued the five-century-old Japanese style of basara, meaning 'way too much' and 'wild rebel' but when he was growing up in the 1950s, they simply reflected a working class taste, rougher than the country's sober traditional aesthetics and westernised post-war aspirations'.

The recuperation of street culture in another place – Pop Art – represents an articulation of its suppressed content and continuity with both high culture and the historical past; a reimagining of the fragments which releases their hidden, sedimented meaning in the fantasy form of fashion. As such the 'damaged' fantasies of 'the proletarian context of living...in the real life cycle, they appear fragmented, mixed up with other moments, transposed back and forth with regard to the fantasy harnessed to them' (Kluge and Negt, op. cit., p.35). A more prosaic example would be the earlier mentioned Willis (1977) study linking the various spheres of working class life; the street, locality, work and intergenerational influences which, as fragmented, suppressing the continuities between working class experience and the curriculum, serve to exclude working class pupils from educational opportunities.

The formation of groups inside and outside the hegemonic bloc is examined by Rancière and Bourdieu amongst others. It is to Rancière, via a short excursus on stratification theory that we now turn to discuss the cultural formation of social strata.

From Stratification Theory to Rancière's 'Being Together' and Difference

Translation and social mobility

The Kantian notion of subreption discussed in Chapter 2 provides a way into a consideration of how the translation of groups or individuals between various social strata and social worlds depends on, is situated by, a world in common behind the classification systems, genres of cultural artefacts, and so on.

The world being shifted from serves to ground the world being shifted into. And the consequent reformulation of the latter involves the process that brought this about.[92] The translation into a social group entails a synthesis and hybridisation with the trajectory of the new recruits; it changes to remain the same as is clear from Bourdieu's (1984, pp.298–301) account of social intermediaries and their mediation of 'new' groups. Such translations mark or mediate the translators and the outcome that continues to be supported, reproduced by that process. Translation involves a reconfiguration of the elements involved in discursive functioning of social worlds; some are suppressed whilst others come to the fore but all depend on an underlying process of articulation of different social worlds rather than pure differentiation.

Hence subreption indexes a world in common that lies behind classification as an outcome of translation. The subreptive moment is also one of disruption, a *tremblé du sens,* in Barthes' terms, an undermining of the syllogistic process of subsumption of particulars within a classification scheme; a moment where the particular becomes indifferent to classification and the latter is thereby opened to the specificity of its context, and so receptive to its reconfiguration. It is an aspect of mediation in which both elements come to resemble or have affinity with each other in their undifferentiatedness. Specifically, it is where

---

[92] Halewood (op. cit., p. 29) notes this theme in Whitehead's Process and Reality: 'how an actual entity becomes constitutes what that actual entity is. Its 'being' is constituted by its becoming'.

classification is reconfigured, the subreptive element is thereby translated to a different field of reference via the metaphorisation of the classification; this is a different condensation/displacement of the existing semantic configuration, which centralises an alternative element and hence transforms the whole field of signification. An element that predicated the original central figure has now itself become the subject/topic.

Every translation, as rehearsed earlier, is also a synthesis, an on-going articulation and reconfiguration of social relations. This is evident in the context of vertical translations within social group stratification as Blackburn and Prandy (1997) have argued, following Giddens' (2001) structuration theory. The perspective of economic liberalism (ibid., p.491) with its discrete individuals and groups in conventional social mobility discourse is here replaced by a sense of process where stratification itself is the backdrop to social group translation and hence medium and outcome of the individual's trajectory. As such the logic of stratification is opened up in a way which enables the situated individual to embody, synthesise or operationalise it as a means of access to their class destination. Viewing stratification as a process rather than merely an outcome enables us to see it in its conditions of possibility rather than accepting it as given – a set of fixed, naturalised categories. Here stratification is seen in its context of coproduction by formal education, the market, division of labour, the contractual-juridical framework of the state, the family, cultural intermediaries, and so on. In other words, taking stratification in its moment of operationalisation enables us to locate the coordination of interrelations or teamwork involved in its construction. In this way, we can gain an understanding of mobility or translation not just between 'given' groupings but as a condition of those groupings themselves; we have an overview of the synchronous, 'systemic' aspect of social translations.

The suppression of this synthesising moment and the homogenising of social strata into discrete groups is, arguably, not merely a lapse in social analysis but reflects the dual ontological character of stratification. On the one hand, groups appear as discrete and homogeneous rather than as a hierarchical continuum, whilst on the other, as in Blackburn and Prandy's work, there appears to be a continuum and group membership is seen as diverse rather homogeneous. The conclusion seems to be that both these perceptions are right but are so because they address different ontological aspects of stratification, albeit that Blackburn and Prandy appear to capture the life chances of concrete individuals more closely. The conventional approach looks at occupational groups and takes an abstractional (*homo clausus*) view of individuals and their life chances via their occupancy of formal institutional roles whilst the Blackburn and Prandy approach is more ethnographic and includes viewing life chances through concrete social connections. The ontological distinction between lived social relations and formal institutional roles although not made by the latter, would seem to follow from their analysis.

The intersubjective, processual moment of interrelation features as a void in class relations thinking, 'a featureless landscape' (ibid., p.493), a suppression of the continuities of lived experience, continuities expressed for instance in Giddens' time-space distanciation, in the lives of working class youth and in Sartre's serial totalisation of the bus queue. The class influence is also, as suggested above, an entailment of the abstractional nature of work in formal institutions. Blackburn and Prandy (op. cit., p.491) mention the dominance of 'liberal individualism' and its 'ideological assumptions' in social mobility analysis and this would seem to function as a performative reflection of the process of stratification itself where, as the writers suggest, sociological analysis and ideology merge.

Rancière: partages du sensible

We now return to the loss of experience of the whole *(Ehfrahung)* in Rancière's account of the division of experience on a class cultural basis, the *partages du sensible* which is paralleled in important ways in the above discussion, the division of the social into discrete groups with concomitant cultural practices which suppresses the links or intersubjective, performative content that connects groups and also individuals and groups. Rancière's (2011, p. 12) point is that the impact of the 'partages' is double-edged, on the one hand it parcels out the cultural skills and knowledge but that this process also entails a commonality in what lies behind the parcelling, that is, the world in common that has to logically pre-exist any parcelling of it.[93] The underlying logic of the

---

[93] It is possible to understand the 'sensory fabric of being together' as an unarticulated logic of coordination of say, the production process that shapes each stage or partage. The underlying unity of the division of labour can therefore be seen as imbricated in this invisible processual logic. These 'networks and interconnections which make up a society' (Clements, op. cit., p.77) can be disrupted, made visible and 'politics is about the transformation of the sensory fabric of 'being together' (see Rancière, 2011, cited

division of labour is that of inclusion/exclusion from the polity, it determines who, is authorised to speak.

> Having a particular 'occupation'…determines the ability or inability to take charge of what is common to the community; it defines what is visible or not in a common space, endowed with a common language, etc. (loc. cit.).

The logic of domination and legitimation as a division of knowledge is argued to be inherent to culture and the aesthetic work and thus a grasp of the work as representing, amongst other things, a situated totality of power relations is a rendering visible of the interconnections of the social. For Rancière, cultural products which are most likely to facilitate this are those which challenge the 'partages' as settled genres through cross-genre forms of subreption.

Hallward usefully encapsulates Rancière's politics of aesthetics as follows:

> The basic argument that recurs throughout Rancière's work is … one that pits the presumptions of a disruptive equality against the advocates of an orderly, hierarchical inequality. Rancière's most general effort has always been to explore the various resources of displacement, indistinction, dedifferentiation, or de-qualification that are available in any given field. That 'everyone thinks' means that they think in the absence of any necessary link between who they are and the roles they perform or the places they occupy; everyone thinks through the freedom of their own self-disassociation (Hallward, 2009, p.141).

Hence, *inter alia,* Jacques Rancière takes up the question of subsumption in a capitalist division of labour as how this affects the capacity for self-representation of differing social groups. Rancière (op. cit., p.15) sees the process of representation as captured ideally in aesthetic forms such as the Greek chorus, dance or spoken poetry although, as Hallward (loc. cit.) notes, this can also be taken as a metaphorical staging. What distinguishes these aesthetic forms is the way they combine the different aspects of representation; representation is a production/outcome but it is also an embodied process, a point that is explicit in these forms. The Greek chorus as Aristotle[94] argues is not only commenting

---

below in this section).

[94] Aristotle (1934) (ed. Moxon), Ch. XX1, p.37: 'The chorus should be considered as one

on an unfolding drama but is also part of that action. Representation is therefore not just a classification but has a performativity which combines identification with the processes that bring it about. It follows that representation cannot be true to its topic if it is split off from its performativity. Abstraction in the division of labour has just this effect, it homogenises groups, as argued above, thus denying them self – expression as unique and diverse subjects. Sense, the expression or enactment of a state of affairs, and reference or identity are thereby divorced.

The 'partages' of the division have a double aspect: they indicate the boundaries of what can be said or written, thought etc. but in doing so they also indicate a content that cannot be expressed the 'what' that is bounded or divided (Rancière, 2005, pp. 12–13). Hence the logic of division is obversely the outline logic of interconnection, the suppressed common language and 'sensory fabric'. This is revealed by disruption of boundaries wherein arguably, following the argument of this text, the object represented appears as both particular and general and this vacillates between being partitioned off, particular to an authorised group of speakers, and being universally accessible. Here interpellation or subjectification of the subject or work fails, is disrupted; the latter becomes indifferent to the would-be subsuming representation, an 'equality of indifference' (Rancière, 2011, p.14). He gives examples of the novel and artworks that challenge genre classification and the inscriptions of capital (both economic and cultural) where 'the regimes of art are dominated and structured by class' (Clements, 2008, p.77). This line of thought is reminiscent of Barthes' (1998, pp.4–6) idea of the 'classic text' or reading, which closes down the polivocity of the text through 'literary' institutional appropriation; it denies the dialogical quality of the text. For Rancière (op. cit., pp.14–15), this dialogical nature of reading entails a fundamental equality amongst its audience, an entitlement to think and speak as much as others.[95]

---

of the persons in the drama; should be a part of the whole, and share in the action.'

[95] As Hallward (p.141) notes: 'everyone thinks' isn't very far from Sartre's familiar account of conscious freedom as indeterminate being for itself, or as discussed earlier, Sartre and Beauvoir's 'one amongst others'. See Sartre (1998), pp. 380–81: 'indifference towards others' involves an 'implicit comprehension of being for others' whilst at the same time 'I am in no way conscious of the fact that the other's look can fix my possibilities and my body'. However, Rancière's focus on a primordial moment of equality also resonates with Beauvoir's view of conflictual intersubjectivity as involving

Yet what is this indifference after all if not the very equality of everything that comes to pass on a written page, available as it is to everyone's eyes? This equality destroys all of the hierarchies of representation and also establishes a community of readers as a community without legitimacy, a community formed only by the random circulation of the written word. In this way, a sensible politicity exists that is immediately attributed to the major forms of aesthetic distribution such as the theatre, the page, or the chorus.

Such an indifference to classification means that subsuming discourses appear as particular, situated rather than universal and this renders a common language of dissensus visible as arguably, the heterogeneous sensory fabric of the everyday where the particularity of forms of representation hitherto deemed to be universal becomes apparent – as belonging to one discourse amongst others. Here, beyond the 'partages' of objectified discourse the sub-text or context of connections across the social spectrum is made visible as a unity of dissensus. A sense of this world or 'being in common' is, for Rancière (2008, pp.3–4), key to participation in a democratic polity.[96]

What the artist does is weave a new sensory fabric by tearing percepts and affects out (*sic*) the perceptions and affections that constitute the fabric of ordinary experience. Weaving this new fabric means creating a form of common expression, or a form of expression of the community. What is common is 'sensation'. The human beings are tied together by a certain sensory fabric, I would say a certain distribution of the sensible, which defines their way of being together and politics is about the transformation of the sensory fabric of the 'being together'.

---

equality and reciprocity, which is absent from Sartre's account in Being and Nothingness. See also Kruks (1990, p.100) on this point.

[96] The discussion of appropriation in Ch. 4 outlined how Amerindians assimilated Christianity to their own belief systems. This requires an understanding of the logics of the two systems and their points of overlap, a sense of a common logic. This is, arguably, a way of grasping Rancière's 'being in common'. Here also the parties are not on an equal footing otherwise.

Civil Society – A Way Forward?

As Rancière notes, the community of dissensus works because its goals are imagined and polyvocal rather than objectifications of its practices. This allows a democratic equality of the dissensus which is framed by an indifference to hierarchies of, in his case, aesthetic reception. This model could be generalised, as suggested above, to a 'theatrocracy' or staging of politics (Hallward, 2009, pp.141–2).

The groupings and movements of civil society in Weber's (2005) open source network account match this democratic equality in their transgression of the formal hierarchies of capitalist modernity as something like a mode of 'being together'.[97]

The open source networks model of civil society was examined earlier and, in the light of Rancière it is worth revisiting briefly some of the themes and issues around the situating of civil society as a genus for non-abstractional social relations within modern social formations.

Rancière argued that 'being together' is essentially a disruptive force which makes connections and forms of misrecognition visible. Hallward (2005, p.41) notes Rancière's 'investments in the liminal thematics of the 'interval' and the 'between', of the hybrid, the indeterminate, the uncertain and so on' which suggests an affinity with the disruptive intersubjectivity outlined in this text. However, his position also seems to suggest that any translation of the sensible/perception to a new field of reference, social world, would result in new forms of hierarchical authority and misrecognition; his politics of interruption 'appears to suspend all forms of authority and authorisation' (Hallward, 2009, p.156).

By contrast, Weber's network structure of open source I.T. suggested a kind of politics that avoids this pitfall in that the configuration and refiguration of networks offers an example of discursively organised social relations that mirrors the metaphorisation aspects of the discursive. Weber's account

---

[97] Civil society is seen here as the domain of contestation of the hegemonic bloc, the domain that defends a sense of equality and reciprocity as against the interests of capital and the formal institutional apparatus of the state. Gramsci's (1971, p.262) account which makes a veiled reference to Marx's 'withering away of the state' is also suggestive here: civil society as the ethical state '(based on the premise that all men are really equal and hence equally rational and moral, i.e. capable of accepting the law freely, and not through coercion, as imposed by another class, as something external to consciousness)'.

demonstrated the performativity of social relations. Aspects of process feed into outcomes and outcomes feed back into process as reconfiguration of the network in ways that are not predictable or closed in the manner of a syllogism as with linear causality of hierarchical ordering. They rather result from the co-existence and coproduction of process and outcome. In other words, it offers the possibility of formations that remain open and dynamic and therefore provides a form of translation which could assuage Rancière's fears.

6

Afterword

The gaps presented in formal institutional discourse by the suppression of the concrete, lived world through which it is operationalised in the here and now in the hegemony of formal institutions are, as we've argued, in fact constitutive of the latter. In reality, formal discourse renders this lived everyday reality as its other or non-being, something aberrant. This 'constitutive outside', to use Jessop's (2006, p.165) term is the absent ground of the abstractional in an ontological dualism of abstractional and lived worlds. The abstractional is, to adapt Arthur's approach, a domain of being and signification without concrete content which itself equivalences concrete things and individuals, according to its own logic and categories, those of capital and the state. This sense of equivalencing is evident in the work of Lukács but also that of Foucault, particularly his observations on hierarchical observation and the examination from *Discipline and Punish.*

The formal institutional hierarchy and its corollary, the isolated individual or *homo clausus* of economic liberalism, were seen to exemplify the abstractional logic of modern capitalism as a homogenisation of social groups as discrete occupational categories containing isolated individuals.

Hence whilst formal institutions are commonly taken as the necessary structural fabric of social life it has been argued here, following Arthur, Habermas, Lefebvre *et al.* that they are in fact ontologically derivative. There is a displacement of their lived, concrete constitutive element, which involves its colonisation and the substitution of abstractions which mimic the lived world displaced, a surreptitious process which leads to the 'inconspicuous' presence of modern capitalism within the concrete lifeworld (Habermas, 1999, p174). The suppression of the subjectivity and intersubjectivity of living subjects entailed by this colonisation was also suggested in various ways in the work of writers as diverse as Barthes, Lukács, Foucault, Negt, Kluge and Rancière.

Networks suggest an alternative to the bifurcation between on the one hand, the interaction of individuals and groups on a peer basis and on the other, the contractual relations and equivalencing of formal relations. As with Open Source, the network functions on the basis of collaboration where in a given context anyone is authorised to speak and authority is conferred by collective consent. Networks entail reciprocal recognition and also recognition in the form of conferred authority, reflecting Beauvoir's model of interrelation where one is both 'one amongst others' and also different, unique (transcending the encounter) in one's recognised capacities. Again, recognition is not just about an agent's role but concerns the performative aspect-role as process, rather than as reproductive aim or outcome of the activity seen as a discrete entity. Here role is in on-going modification via interrelation with the 'team'. It's worth noting that the network model of organisation with its emphasis on recognition and reciprocity crops up ironically, in management discourse[98], as a way of handling fluid situations, problem solving, uncertainty, commitment and so on. According to Burns and Stalker (1961, p.105) this requires

…The adjustment and continual re-definition of individual tasks through interaction with others…

A network structure of control, authority, and communication. The sanctions which apply to the individual's conduct in his (*sic*) working role derive more from presumed community of interest with the rest of the working organisation in the survival and growth of the firm, and less from a contractual relationship between himself (*sic*) and a non-personal corporation, represented for him by an immediate superior.

Omniscience no longer imputed to the head of the concern; knowledge about the technical or commercial nature of the here and now task may be located anywhere in the network; this location becoming the ad hoc centre of control authority and communication.

The effect of formal institutional 'life' it has been argued, is to displace this 'network' content such that it is not engaged with in its lived place. It is not seen

---

[98] Burns and Stalker are concerned here primarily with optimising a firm's output under changing conditions.

as the taken for granted, ground of institutional practice but as something that is institutionally initiated, it is as if it appears *ex nihilo*. Hence it is a specific kind of non-being, one that swallows its actual grounds such that the gaps in formal discourse are naturalised. On the other hand, the form of non-being identified as consonant with non-abstractional relations here is that of the ground or threshold of being. The problem with real abstraction is that one form of non-being stands in for the other in a surreptious way, derives its life from something else, that is, the operationalisation of formal structures is something accomplished but this genesis cannot be recognised as such within formal discourse. The structures of the latter are then not merely objectifications of social relations but naturalisations of them – relations and their entities as discrete existents. The solution suggested here was to regard objectification or identification as a process rather than purely an outcome, to see identity as manifested in say, the urban environment as always subject to its journey as metaphorical transfer or translation and as such containing an essential hybridity, there to be articulated. As argued earlier, when the urban environment becomes an abstraction, commodified practices can be seen as a physically experienced and embodied form of estrangement.

Other areas in which abstraction could be pursued as a research topic include the psycho-social where the suppression of the subject in formal discourse can be seen in terms of how abstractions are internalised as negations of being, things that threaten the integrity of the subject. These manifest themselves as part objects, fetishes where a category or predicate becomes the thing or topic itself as in the case of the 'thing-category' of the stereotype; something at once projected onto others and an enduring part of the psyche. Institutional definitions of the individual arguably gain a purchase in this way. Again, in the sphere of the phenomenology of the body, the individual is subject to a sense that it is the parts that are real, more real than the experience of embodiment which is itself displaced into the parts of the body. These then become the focus of desire or dislike as in the obsession with bodily appearance. The novelist Rooney captures this in *Conversations with Friends*.

My body felt completely disposable, like a placeholder for something more valuable. I fantasised about taking it apart and lining my limbs up side by side to compare them (Rooney, 2017, p.286).

Here Rooney encapsulates the effects of commodification of the body[99] and its colonisation in a critical way. The sensuous, lived body is experienced as estrangement. Following Benjamin (Khatib, 2013, pp. 2, 4 and 8) a corollary of the disintegration of this phantasmagoric[100] body, its 'deformation', is the suggestion of a *Gestalt* or logic of its assembly, how it is put together. The colonisation of embodied being has to be operationalised from pure abstraction to situated life. The dissolution of this *Gestalt* image likewise involves a sense of the logic involved. In Rooney's case, this sense is conveyed through the parodic way in which the estranged body is experienced (*Phantasie*) as an assemblage of limbs to be compared. The entertainment of the parodic entails a sense of the topic to be parodied. A similar operation was identified in de Certeau's account of how Amerindians appropriated Christianity. Further, as Sandford has noted, the political promise of this situation can be realised when not only do we have a sense of the logic of the colonisation but can contest it and translate or articulate it in terms of a different and liberatory field of reference and its social world.

Phenomenological social theory enables a grasp of the moment of deformation, as evidenced from Benjamin's use of its ideas. The open horizontal mode of perception of everyday life (apperception) de-differentiates abstractions from what they subsume because within a given situation it makes no distinction between the category and the thing categorised, everything appears on the same plane and, in other words, is subject to the criticism of everyday life. Here the empty categories of commodity exchange are presented with their external/estranged contents as having an autonomy or indifference which subverts the grip of abstraction's subsuming externality on its contents.

---

[99] Although these experiences seem to be particular to the subject, the interpellation process depends on the hiatus created by the suppression of the intersubjective content, the mediation of an abstractional culture as the lived reality of individual lives.

[100] Khatib (op. cit., p. 4) suggests that phantasmagoric phenomena are not 'mere illusions… [rather they are] a certain type of phenomena which acquire a material density within capitalist everyday life… [not purely ideological] but designate an objective content in relation to a commodified mode of perception… [they] are not representations but immediate images…"data" of "quasi-perceptions" within the reality of the commodity form'. Khatib notes Benjamin's use of Husserl's 'phantasms' here – a reality sensed, intimated but not yet identified, which in Benjamin can take a material guise within the abstractions of the commodity form.

Bibliography

Adorno, T.W. (trans. E.B. Ashton) (1973), *Negative Dialectics*, Routledge and Kegan Paul, London.

Arthur, C.J. (2001), 'The Spectral Ontology of Value', *Radical Philosophy* 107, May/June, pp. 32–42.

Bakhtin, M. (1981), *The Dialogical Imagination*, University of Texas, Austin.

Barbaras, R. (trans, T. Toadvine and L. Lawlor) (1994), *The Being of the Phenomenon: Merleau-Ponty's Ontology,* Indiana University Press, Bloomington and Indianopolis.

Barbaras, R. (trans. P.B. Milan) (2006), *Desire and Distance: Introduction to a Phenomenology of Perception*, Stanford University Press, Stanford, Ca.

Barthes, R. (1977), *Image, Music, Text*, Fontana Press/Harper Collins, London.

Barthes, R. (1994), *Empire of Signs*, Hill and Wang/Farrar, Straus and Giroux, New York.

Barthes, R. (2004), (trans. R. Miller), *S/Z,* Basil Blackwell, Oxford.

Blackburn, R.M. and Prandy, K. (1997), 'The Reproduction of Social Inequality', *Sociology*, Vol. 31, No. 3, August, pp.491–510.

de Beauvoir, S. (1944), *Pyrrhus et Cineas,* Gallimard, Paris.
de Beauvoir, S. (1972) (trans. and ed. H.M. Parshley), *The Second Sex*, Penguin Books Ltd., Harmondsworth, U.K. and Victoria, Australia.

de Beauvoir, S. (trans. P. O'Brian) (1988), *Adieux: A Farewell to Sartre*, Penguin Books, London and Harmondsworth.

Benjamin, W. (trans. H. Eiland and K. McLaughlin) (1999), *The ArcadesProject*, Belknap/Harvard, Cambridge, Mass. and London.

Bhandar, B. and Toscano, A. (2015), 'Race, Real Estate and Real Abstraction', *Radical Philosophy* 194, Nov/Dec. pp. 8–17.

Bordo, S. (1993), *Unbearable Weight: Feminism, Western Culture and the Body*, University of California Press, Berkeley, Los Angeles and London.

Bourdieu, P. (trans. R. Nice) (1984), *Distinction: A Social Critique of the Judgement of Taste*, Routledge, London,

Bourdieu, P. (1992), *Language and Symbolic Power*, Polity Press, Cambridge.

Bourdieu, P. (2006), *Outline of a Theory of Practice*, Cambridge University Press, Cambridge.

Buck-Morss, S. (1990), *The Dialectics of Seeing: Walter* Benjamin and *the Arcades Project*, The M.I.T. Press, Cambridge, Mass. and London.

Burrow, C. (2015), 'What is a Pikestaff?': Review of D. Donoghue (2014), *Metaphor* (Harvard), London Review of Books, Vol.37, No. 8, 23rd April, p.27.

Burns, T. and Stalker, G.M. (1961), *The Management of Innovation*, Tavistock, London.

Callon, M. and Latour, B. (1981), 'Unscrewing the Big Leviathan: How Actors Macro-Structure Reality and How Sociologists Help Them to do so', in K. Knorr-Cetina and V. Cicourel (eds*.) Advances in Social Theory and Methodology: Towards an Integration of Micro- and Macro-Sociologies*, Routledge and Kegan Paul, London, pp.277–303.

Carter, S. T. Jordan, T. and Watson, S. (2008), Introduction in S, Clarke, T. Jordan and S. Watson (eds.), *Security: Sociology and Social Worlds*, Manchester University Press, Manchester and New York.

Carl, W. (1994), *Frege's Theory of Sense and Reference: its Origins and Scope*, Cambridge University Press, Cambridge and New York.

de Certeau, M. (1984), *The Practice of Everyday Life*, University of California Press, L.A. and London.

Clarke, A. (1997), 'A social worlds research adventure: the case of reproductive science' in A. Strauss and J. Corbin (eds.), *Grounded Theory in Practice*, Sage, London.

Clements, P. (2017), *The Creative Underground: Art, Politics and Everyday Life*, Routledge, New York and London.

Cohen, S. (1972), *Folk Devils and Moral Panics: the Creation of the Mods and Rockers*, Paladin/Granada Publishing, St Albans, Herts.

Crist, M. (2018), 'Race Doesn't Come into It', Letters: *London Review of Books*, 25th Oct., p 4.

Cuff, E.C., Sharrock, W.W., and Francis, D.W. (1992), *Perspectives in Sociology*, Routledge, London and New York.

Davies, T. (1989), 'Education, Ideology and Literature' in T. Bennett, G. Martin, C. Mercer and J. Woollacott (eds.), *Culture, Ideology and Social Process*, The Open University, London, pp. 251–260.

Debord, G. (1983), *Society of the Spectacle*, Rebel Press/Dark Star, London.
Delphy, C. (1991), 'Penser le Genre: Quels Problemes?' in M-C. Hurtig *et al.*, *Sexe et Genre: de la Hierarchie entre les Sexes,* Editions du Centre National de la Recherche Scientifique, Paris.

Delphy, C. (trans. D. Leonard) (1993), 'Rethinking Sex and Gender', *Women's Studies International Forum,* vol. 16, no. 1, pp. 1–9.

Derrida, J. (trans. F.C.T. Moore) (1974), 'White Mythology', *New Literary History,* 6, Vol. 1, pp. 5–74.

Derrida, J. (trans. G.C. Spivak) (1976), *Of Grammatology*, Johns Hopkins University Press, Baltimore, Maryland.

Derrida, J. (trans. A. Bass) (1982), *Margins of Philosophy*, University of Chicago Press, Chicago.

Derrida, J. (1994) (trans. P. Kamuf), *Specters of Marx: the State of the Debt and the Work of Mourning*, Routledge.

Dorlin, E. (2008), *Sexe, Genre et Sexualites*, PUF, Paris.

Dummett, M. (1981), *The Interpretation of Frege's Philosophy*, Harvard University Press, Cambridge, Mass.

Dummett, M. (1994), *The Logical Basis of Metaphysics*, Harvard University Press, Cambridge, Mass.

Duroux, Y. (2012b), 'Strong Structuralism, Weak Subject: An Interview with Yves Duroux', in P. Hallward and K. Peden (eds.), *Concept and Form, Vol. 2: Interviews and Essays on the Cahiers pour L'Analyse*, Verso, London and N.Y., pp. 187–202.

Eagleton, T. (1975), 'Ideology and Literary Form', *New Left Review* No. 90, March-April, pp.81–109.

Elias, N. (2000), *The Civilizing Process: Sociogenetic and Psychogenetic Investigations*, Blackwell Publishing, Oxford

Fanon, F. (trans. C. Farrington) (1971), *The Wretched of the Earth*, Penguin Books, Harmondsworth.

Fanon, F. (trans. C.L. Markmann) (1973), *Black Skin, White Masks*, Paladin/ Granada Publishing, St Albans, Herts.

Feather, H. (2000), *Intersubjectivity and Contemporary Social Theory: the Everyday as Critique,* Ashgate, Aldershot

Feather, H. (2016), 'Antinomialism in the Social Sciences'. Review of S. Susen, *'The Postmodern Turn' in the Social Sciences, Journal of Political Power,* Vol. 9, Issue 2, pp. 327–333.

Feuerbach, L. (1987), 'Towards a Critique of the Hegelian Philosophy', in L.S. Steppelvitch (ed. & intro.), *The Young Hegelians*, Cambridge University Press, Cambridge.

Fisher, M. (2009), *Capitalist Realism: Is There No Alternative?*, Zero Books, Winchester, U.K. and Washington, U.S.

Foucault, M. (1984), *The History of Sexuality: An Introduction*, Peregrine Books, Harmondsworth.

Foucault, M. (trans. A.M. Sheridan Smith) (1982), *The Archaeology of Knowledge*, Tavistock Publications, London.

Foucault, M. (1986), 'Disciplinary Power and Subjection', in S. Lukes (ed.) *Power,* Basil Blackwell, Oxford, pp. 229–242.

Foucault, M. (1999), 'The Means of Correct Training', in A. Elliott (ed.) *The Blackwell Reader in Contemporary Social Theory*, Blackwell Publications, Oxford.

Frege, G. (trans. P. Long, R. White and R. Hargreaves) (1979), *Posthumous Writings*, Blackwell, Oxford.

Garfinkel, H. (1967), *Studies in Ethnomethodology*, Prentice Hall, Engelwood Cliffs.

du Gay, P. *et al.* (1997), 'Making Sense of the Walkman', in P. du Gay, S. Hall, L. James, H. Mackay and K. Negus, *Doing Cultural Studies: the Story of the Sony Walkman,* Sage publications in association with the Open University, London, Thousand Oaks & New Delhi.

du Gay, P. (2008), 'Organising Conduct, Making Up People', in L. McFall, P. du Gay and S. Carter (eds.), *Conduct: Sociology and Social Worlds*, Manchester University Press, Manchester and New York.

Giddens, A. (2001), *The Constitution of Society: Outline of the Theory of Structuration*, Polity Press, Cambridge.

Goffman, I. (1982), *The Presentation of Self in Everyday Life*, Penguin Books, Harmondsworth.

Goldberg, D. (1997), *Racial Subjects: Writing on Race in America*, Routledge, New York.

Gramsci, A. (1971) (trans. H. Eiland and K. McLaughlin), *Selections from Prison Notebooks*, Lawrence and Wishart, London.

Guardian, The (2001), 'Black Tory peer puts Hague on the spot in race row', April 28th, p. 4.

Habermas, J. (1999), 'The Uncoupling of System and Lifeworld', in (A. Elliot ed.), *The Blackwell Reader in Contemporary Social Theory*, Blackwell Publishers, Oxford.

Halewood, M. (2013), *A.N. Whitehead and Social Theory: Tracing a Culture of Thought*, Anthem Press, London.

Hall, S. (1997), 'The Spectacle of the Other' in S. Hall (ed.) *Representation: Cultural Representations and Signifying Practices*, Sage in association with the Open University, London, Thousand Oaks, L.A., and New Delhi.

Hallward, P. (2005), 'Jacques Ranciere and the Subversion of Mastery', *Paragraph*, Vol. 28, Issue 1, pp.26–45.

Hallward, P. (2009), 'Staging Equality: Ranciere's Theatrocracy and the Limits of Anarchic Equality' in G. Rockhill and P. Watts (eds.), *History, Politics, Aesthetics*, Duke University Press, E-Duke Books Scholarly Collection, Durham N. Carolina.

Harvey, D. (2006), 'Space as a Keyword', in N. Castree & D. Gregory (eds.) *David Harvey: A Critical Reader*, Blackwell Publishing, Oxford and Malden, M.A., pp. 270–93.

Harvey, D. (2010), *The Enigma of Capital and the Crises of Capitalism,* Profile Books Ltd., London.

Harvey, D. (2012), *Rebel Cities: From the Right to the City to the Urban Revolution,* Verso Books, London.

Hegel, G.W.F. (trans. T.M. Knox) (1942), *Hegel's Philosophy of Right*, The Clarendon Press, Oxford.

Hegel, G.W.F. (trans and intro. J. Baillie) (1966), *The Phenomenology of Mind*, George Allen & Unwin Ltd., London.

Hobsbawm, J. (2012), 'It's not what you know but who – the return of an unfortunate reality', *The Guardian*, June 30th, p.43.

Hoens, D. (2014), 'Red Carnation': review of Hallward P. and Peden, K., (eds.) *Concept and Form* (2012), op. cit., *Radical Philosophy* 183, pp. 47–50.
Holloway, J. (2010), *Crack Capitalism*, Pluto Press, London.
Horwell, V. (2020), 'Kansai Yamamoto: fashion designer who created stage outfits for stars including David Bowie and Lady Gaga', *The Guardian,* Journal: Obituaries, 1st Aug., p.6.

Husserl, E. (1970) (ed. and trans. D. Carr), *The Crisis of the European Sciences and Transcendental Phenomenology*, Northwestern University Press, Evanston.

Irigaray, l. (trans. C. Porter) (1985), *This Sex Which is Not One*, Cornell University Press, Ithaca, New York.

Jameson, F. (foreword, N. Larsen) (1989), *The Ideologies of Theory: Essays 1971–1986, Volume 1, Situations of Theory*, University of Minnesota Press, Ma.

Jameson, F. (1991), *Postmodernism or the Cultural Logic of Late Capitalism*, Verso, London.

Jessop, B (2006), 'Spatial Fixes, Temporal Fixes, and Spatio-Temporal Fixes', in (B. Castree and D. Gregory eds) *David Harvey: A Critical Reader*, Blackwell publishing, Malden, MA and Oxford.

Kant, I. (trans. N. Kemp Smith) (1976), *Immanuel Kant's Critique of Pure Reason*, The Macmillan Press Ltd., London and Basingstoke.

Kelion, L. (2012), 'Linus Torvalds: Linux succeeded thanks to selfishness and trust', https://www.bbc.co.uk/news/technology-18419231(accessed 10.6.2019).

Khatib, S. (2013), 'Fantasy, Phantasmagoria and Image-Space. Walter Benjamin's Politics of Pure Means'. Paper presented at the conference series 'Die Politik des Phantasmas' Vol. 5: 'Phantasma und Politik', at Hebble am Ufer Theatre, Berlin, Nov. 23rd 2013. Available at: *www.Academia.edu/527726/Fantasy_phantasmagoria_und_pmage*-Space. Accessed 1/10/19.

Khatib, S. (2016), Review of A. Gelley (2015), *Benjamin's Passages – Dreaming, Awakening, The Germanic Review: Literature, Culture, Theory*, Vol. 91, issue 2, pp. 199–206.

Khatib, S. (2017), 'Sensuous Supersensuous: The Aesthetics of Real Abstraction', in S. Gandsha and J. Hartle (eds.), *Aesthetic Marx*, Bloomsbury, London, pp. 49–72.

Kraniauskas, J. (2014), 'Rhetorics of Populism: Ernesto Laclau, 1935–2014', *Radical Philosophy* 186, Jul/Aug, pp. 29–36.

Kruks, S. (1990), *Situation and Human Existence: Freedom, Subjectivity and Society*, Unwin Hyman, London.

Laclau, E. (2014), *The Rhetorical Foundations of Society*, Verso, London and New York.

Laing, R.D. and Cooper, D.G. (preface J.-P. Sartre) (1964), *Reason and Violence: A Decade of Sartre's Philosophy 1950–1960,* Tavistock Publications, London.

Laqueur, T. (1990), *Making Sex: Body and Gender from the Greeks to Freud*, Harvard University Press, Cambridge, MA.

Latour, B. (1987), *Science in Action: How to Follow Scientists and Engineers Through Society*, Open University Press, Buckingham.

Lefebvre, H. (2002a), (trans. S. Rabinovitch), *Everyday Life in the Modern World*, Continuum, N.Y. and London.

Lefebvre, H.(2002b), (trans. J. Moore), *Critique of Everyday Life, Vol. 2,* Verso, London and N.Y.

Leiberknecht, O. *et al.* (2019), Discussion: 'Homo Clausus', https://de.wikipedia.org/wiki/Homo_Clausus (accessed 12.06.19).

Leslie, E. (2000), *Walter Benjamin: Overpowering Conformism*, Pluto Press, London, Sterling, Virginia.

Lukács, G. (1971), (trans. R. Livingstone), *History and Class Consciousness: Studies in Marxist Dialectics*, Merlin Press, London.

MacIntyre, A., (2007), *After Virtue: A Study in Moral Theory*, Gerald Duckworth & Co., London.

Marx, K. (1974), *Capital*, Vol.1, Lawrence and Wishart, London.

Marx, K. (intro. E. Mandel & trans. B. Fowkes) (1991), *Capital*, vol. 1, Penguin, Harmondsworth.

Mauss, M. (1973), 'Techniques of the Body', *Economy and Society*, vol. 2, no. 1, pp.70–88.

Mead, G. H. (1970), *Mind, Self and Society*, University of Chicago Press, London.

Mensch, J. (2013), *Kant's Organicism: Epigenesis and the Development of Critical Philosophy*, Chicago University Press, Chicago.

Mercer, K., (1994), *Welcome to the Jungle; New Positions in Black Cultural Studies*, Routledge, New York and London.

Mercer, K. (1995), 'Busy in the Ruins of Wretched Phantasia', in R. Farr (ed.) *Mirage: Images of Race, Difference and Desire*, Institute of Contemporary Arts, London.

Merleau-Ponty, M. (1964), (trans. and preface H.L. Dreyfus and P.A. Dreyfus) *Sense and Non-Sense*, Northwestern University Press, Evanston.

Merleau-Ponty, M. (1992a), (ed. and intro. J.M. Edie) *The Primacy of Perception*, Northwestern University Press, Evanston.

Merleau-Ponty, M. (1992b), (trans. A. Lingis and ed. C. Lefort) *The Visible and the Invisible*, Northwestern University Press, Evanston.

Merleau-Ponty, M. (1998), (trans. and intro. R.C. McCleary), *Signs*, Northwestern University Press, Evanston.

Merleau-Ponty, M. (2001), (trans. J. O'Neill), *Humanisn and Terror: an Essay on the Communist Problem*, Beacon Press, Boston, Mass.

Metcalf, S. (2017), 'The Big Idea that Defines our Era', The Long Read: Journal, *The Guardian,* 19th Aug., pp. 29–32.

Miller, J.-A. (2012a), 'Suture (Elements of the Logic of the Signifier)' in P. Hallward and K. Peden (eds.) *Concept and Form, Vol. 1, Selections from the Cahiers pour l'Analyse*, Verso, London and New York.

McNulty, T. (2012b), 'Desuturing Desire: The Work of the Letter in the Mille-Leclaire Debate', in Hallward and Peden (eds.) op. cit.

Moos, M. (2015), *Breaking the Silence: Voices of the British Children of Refugees from Nazism*, Rowman & Littlefield International.

Mouzelis, N. (1995), *Sociological Theory: What Went Wrong; Diagnosis and Remedies*, Routledge, London and New York.

Negt, O. and Kluge, A. (Foreward M. Hansen)(2016), *Public Sphere and Experience: Toward an Analysis of the Bourgeois and Proletarian Public Sphere*, Verso, London and New York.

Osborne, P. (1995), *The Politics of Time: Modernity and the Avant-Garde*, Verso, London and New York.

Parker, J. (2000), *Structuration,* Open University Press, Buckingham and Philadelphia.

Potts, R. (2016), 'Smirk Host Panegyric: J.H. Prynne': a Review of J.H. Prynne (2015), *Poems* (Bloodaxe), *London Review of Books*, Vol. 38, No. 11, 2nd June, pp. 16–17.

Puwar, N. (2001), 'The Racialised Somatic Norm and the Senior Civil Service', *Sociology* 35 (3), pp. 651–70.

Puwar, N. (2004), *Space Invaders: Race, Gender and Bodies Out of Place*, Berg, Oxford and New York.

Rancière, J. (2008), 'Aesthetic Separation, Aesthetic Community: Scenes from the Aesthetic Regime of Art', Art & Research: A Journal of ideas, Contexts and Methods.

Rancière, J. (2011) (trans. and intro. G. Rockhill), *The Distribution of the Sensible*, Continuum International Publishing Group, London and New York.

Redman, P. (2008), 'Afterword', in P. Redman (ed.) *Attachment: Sociology and Social Worlds*, Manchester University Press, Manchester, pp. 175–184.

Riceour, P. (1986), (trans. R. Czerny), *The Rule of Metaphor: Multidisciplinary studies of the creation of meaning in language,* Routledge and Kegan Paul, London.

Rooney, S, (2017), *Conversations with Friends*, Faber and Faber Ltd., London.

Rowbotham, S. (1973), *Woman's Consciousness, Man's World*, Penguin Books, Harmondsworth.

Russell, B. (1973), 'On Denoting', in D. Lackey (ed.), *Bertrand Russell: Essays in Analysis,* George Allen & Unwin, London, pp.103–119.

Rustin, M. (2008), 'What does Psychoanalysis Contribute to Our Understanding of Failures of Social interconnectedness?' in P. Redman (ed.) *Attachment: Sociology and Social Worlds*, Manchester University Press, Manchester and New York, pp. 143–174.

Sandford, S. (2011), 'Sex: A Transdisciplinary Concept', *Radical Philosophy* 165, Jan/Feb., pp. 23–30.

Sartre, J-P. (1982), *Critique of Dialectical Reason*, Verso/NLB, London.

Sartre, J-P. (1998) (trans. H.E. Barnes, intro. M. Warnock), *Being and Nothingness: An Essay on Phenomenological Ontology*, Routledge, London.

Scarry, E. (1985), *The Body in Pain: the Making and Unmaking of the World*, Oxford University Press, Oxford.

Schutz, A. (1967) (ed. M. Natanson), *The Problem of Social Reality: Collected Papers*, Vol. 1, Martinus Nijhoff, The Hague.

Schutz, A. (1970a), 'Concept and Theory Formation in the Social Sciences', in d. Emmett and A. MacIntyre (eds.) *Sociological Theory and Philosophical Analysis*, Macmillan, London and Basingstoke pp.1–19.

Schutz, A. (1970b), 'The Problem of Rationality in the Social World' in D. Emmett and A. MacIntyre (eds.) (op. cit.), pp.89–114.

Sheppard, E. (2006), 'David Harvey and Dialectical Space-time', in N. Castree & D. Gregory (eds.), *David Harvey: A Critical Reader*, op. cit., pp. 121–141.

Simmel, G. (1978), (trans. T. Bottomore and D. Frisby, and ed. D. Frisby) *The Philosophy of Money*, Routledge and Kegan Paul, London.

Sohn-Rethel, A. (1978), *Intellectual and Manual Labour: a Critique of Epistemology*, Humanities Press, Atlantic Highlands, New Jersey.

Smith, Z. (2009), *Changing My Mind: Occasional Essays*, Penguin Books, London.

Strauss, A. L. (1964), *Psychiatric Ideologies and Institutions*, Free Press.

Strauss, A., (1978), 'A social world perspective', *Studies in Symbolic Interaction,* vol. 1, pp. 119–128.

Sukov, L. (2009), *Homo Clausus: Ein Neidergang*, Culture Machines, Berlin.

Waldron, R.A. (1967), *Sense and Sense Development*, Andre Deutsch, London.

Weber, S. (2005), *The Success of Open Source*, Harvard University Press, Cambridge, Mass. and London.

Weir, A. (2001), 'Do I have to?' *The Guardian Weekend*, April 28th, p.70.

Whitehead, A. N. (2011), *Science and the Modern World*, Cambridge University Press, New York and Cambridge.

Williams, R. (1971), *Culture and Society 1780–1950*, Penguin Books in association with Chatto and Windus, Harmondsworth.

Willis, P. (1977), *Learning to Labour*, Saxon House, Farnborough.

Wilson, E. (1991), *The Sphinx in the City: Urban Life, the Control of Disorder, and Women*, Virago Press, London.

Wittig, M. (1992), 'The Category of Sex' in *The Straight Mind and Other Essays*, Beacon Press, Boston, MA.

Wohlfarth, I. (1996), 'Smashing the Kaleidoscope: Walter Benjamin's Critique of Cultural History', in M.P. Steinberg, *Walter Benjamin and the Demands of History*, Cornell University Press, Ithaca; London, pp.190–205.

Wood, D. (1989), *The Deconstruction of Time*, Contemporary Studies in Philosophy and the Human Sciences, Humanities Press, Atlantic Highlands, N.J.

Wood, M. (2008), 'Marvellous Money', Review of J.M.E. de Queiros, *The Maias: Episodes from Romantic Life*, *London Review of Books*, 3rd Jan., pp. 13–14.

Wood, M. (2017), 'Fritz Lang and the Life of Crime', *London Review of Books*, Vol. 39, No. 8, April 20th, pp.19–22.

Woodward, K. (2008), 'Boxing Masculinities: Attachment, Embodiment and Heroic Practices' in P. Redman (ed.) *Attachment: Sociology and Social Worlds*, Manchester University Press, Manchester, pp.83–110.

Žižek, S. (2014), *Event: Philosophy in Transit,* Penguin Books, London.

Index

www.ingramcontent.com/pod-product-compliance
Lightning Source LLC
Chambersburg PA
CBHW060503290526
45791CB00001B/241